LONDON POLICE DIVERS STO

1983 to 1996

True Stories by Mackenzie Moulton

Who served with the police diving unit for 13 years.

Copyright © Mackenzie Moulton 2020

All rights reserved. No part of this publication may be reproduced, stored in a retrieval system or transmitted in any form or by any means or used for any film, play or video, without the prior written permission of the Author.

Front Cover

Myself, and my good friend and colleague John (Smoothy) Smith, in West India Dock, standing next to a stolen Rolls Royce we had recovered.

It was like a car park down there, with some times 3 cars on top of each other, but only the Rolls Royce was considered recoverable by the Insurance company.

We were originally called to look for a stolen motor cycle, that had been seen to be dumped into the dock.

We found it on the top of the bonnet of one of the many cars.

Contents

Page 5 Police Underwater Search Unit

15 Introduction

20 1983 In the beginning

24 Trapped under a safe 13th June 1984

32 Headless body

39 Gun found in Regents Park 23rd April 1986

42 Merlin 1987

45 Mark Piers RIP 15th February 1989

55 The MV Marchioness disaster 20th August 1989

76 Body in Hampstead ponds 3rd August 1990

82 Water take off tower 19th August 1991

93 Boat child crushed under his home 2nd May 1992

97 Taxi driver found in dock

112 Ships bottom search 14th April 1993

120 Body in Burgess park and body in box
     30th May 1993

126 Two men drown on a sunny day in Denham
     1st May 1994

139 Security search for HRH The Duke of York
     19th May 1994

163 The Well 23rd May 1994

167 The Well continued

175 Enclosed space training 7th June 1994

183 Training for security searches

187 Remand prisoner drowns 20th July 1994

195 Dog bite 29th July 1994

200 Christabel Boyce 1985

Police Underwater Search Unit

The primary role of the police diver is to provide a search facility in support of land based officers investigating all incidents of crime, missing persons and lost property, and to recover anything from coin to ammunition, firearms, weapons, safes to all types of motor vehicles, from cycles to lorries and even heavy plant, and of course, dead bodies.

Other roles included are, assistance in flood situations, security searches, assistance to Customs & Excise, when they need the outside of a vessel searching, elimination searches and inspection and repair of police owned floating property and vessels.

The origins of the police diver date back to 1954, when the first unit was formed in Berkshire, primarily for recovery of dead bodies. Since then the idea has caught on, to deal with things other than bodies, and today there are some 20 units covering the UK, working on a full and part time basis, determined by the workload of each unit.

The police service as I write this book have two diving schools through which each police diver goes on various courses, from basic divers course to supervisors. These schools are at Strathclyde and Sunderland. All police divers are volunteers, who may return to ordinary duty whenever they wish, and are accepted onto a unit, subject to passing the necessary medical and aptitude test.

Units have a search capability to a depth of one hundred and sixty five feet or fifty metres in all types of water, from the open sea to inland lakes, reservoirs, ponds, rivers and canals. They also work in sewers, wells and even water cisterns on top of tower blocks. In other words, if it's wet then a police diver has probably been there.

The Metropolitan Police Underwater Search Unit (USU) is based down-river of Tower Bridge at Wapping Police Station. The unit is 11 strong, and this includes a civilian driver, one inspector, a sergeant and eight constables. The unit gives a seven day a week, twenty-four hour coverage, working a day shift and being on call for the remainder of the time.

The unit has the use of Thames division boats for diving on the River Thames and all members are qualified boat handlers with a department of trade commercial licence, as well as an HSE commercial diver's licence. They have two inflatable boats to enable them to dive and work in almost any locality. The USU has a specially designed fourteen-ton lorry that is equipped to carry three personnel in the front cab and eight in the rear, as well as all their diving equipment.

The main problems for a police diver are, black water, cold, pollution and rubbish, such as barbed wire, hypodermic needles, glass and any other sharp object the diver may not see.

Cold and polluted waters are partially solved by the use of dry diving suits, plenty of thermal undergarments, and a full face mask. As only neoprene-gloved hands come into contact with the water, the risks from pollution and chemical agents are cut right down. Black water and rubbish is only overcome by constant practice and the development of a sensitive sense of touch, overcoming an active imagination and the intelligent use of bottom search lines.

Properly done the police diver expects 100 per cent recovery.

All police divers receive a good grounding in the preserving of evidence in cases of crime, accident or suspected crime, and in complicated cases can call on the assistance of a scenes of crime officer (soco) who deals with the preservation of evidence, including wrapping up to preserve the exhibits. The medium of water will exclude the soco from the location, and the known rules of handling and packaging tend to go out the window, so everything will the depend on the skill and integrity of the police diver, who in most cases will not even see what he is doing, relying only on touch. The diver locating an object by touch must decide whether it is the object wanted or not, and the act of touching brings in the element of cross-contamination, which means the danger of moving microscopic evidence from the article, which will then be lost.

An example: During a killing at a bank robbery, a sawn off shotgun was fired at the glass partition separating customers from the bank teller. The gun was recovered from the river Thames some three months later. Because care was taken by the police diver in the recovery of the gun, the police laboratory found 1150 particles of glass fragments on the weapon, over a hundred of which were in the right hand barrel which had been fired. The finding of those fragments put the gun at the murder scene. Other marks put the gun in the hands of the man subsequently convicted.

Any object recovered from water may well provide forensic evidence. A letter taken from the clothing of a dead body recovered after three weeks immersed in water provided fingerprints by use of laser. A knife, no matter how new or how long in the water, if used in a stabbing will always have a minute blood sample.

In the recovering of a body, never a pleasant job, especially underwater. A diver is concerned with his own safety, currents, lack of visibility and problems caused by disorientation. Wrapping and bagging a body underwater is difficult to say the least, and the main problem is finding enough hands to work with.

Below, the early days of Police diving. There were no health and safety regulations at this time and divers were selected and trained within the Metropolitan Police Thames Division.

The early days of the Metropolitan Police Underwater Search Unit using Navy dry suits and diving equipment.

This picture shows the use of basic surface demand equipment.

The diver has an airline that comes from a large air tank and is attached to his diving regulator. One attendant has his lifeline and the other his airline.

In the background is the standby diver to assist should the main diver searching get trapped.

The diver enters the water down a ladder slowly as he does not know what object may be on the bottom of the canal that could injure him on his descent.

The first Underwater Search Unit (USU) lorry shown alongside a police Wolseley car.

The second USU equipment vehicle was a converted furniture lorry. Fitted with a tow bar, it was able to pull a wooden boat.

This was the lorry newly commissioned for the USU when I was serving.

At the time it was a specially designed purpose built vehicle based on a 14-ton Leyland Lorry with accommodation for 9 personnel

Myself and Jim, both qualified HGV 3, to drive the USU lorry

Introduction

Today is Wednesday 27th June 1990 and it is 7 o'clock in the morning and we, that is the Metropolitan Underwater Search Unit, have just finished searching under a bridge, that crosses a lake in St James Park, central London. It's the Queen's Birthday celebration and the soldiers that will be marching in a parade sometimes use the bridge during dispersal, therefore it has to be checked out to make sure no terrorist organizations have left a bomb attached to the bridge or in the water under the bridge. Once the bridge and the lake have been checked, we are required to stay near the bridge until the ceremony is over and the soldiers are safely back in their barracks.

It was on this occasion, when we had time to spare, I thought I would start to write a book about the interesting work we have done in the Underwater Search Unit, known to all in the Metropolitan Police as the USU

I will briefly tell you about myself.

I was born on 21st June 1947, in Exeter, Devon, UK. I am what they call a baby boomer. I have an English father and a Scottish mother. I spent all my childhood in Devon apart from the occasional visit to my relatives in Scotland.

At quite an early age I was an accomplished artist, and wanted to go to Exeter Art College when I left school, but my father, who was a policeman, advised me against it because there was talk of the students taking drugs at that time, and they were using drugs called purple hearts, and morning glory. So when I left school at 15 years of age, I got a job as a trainee estimator for a local building contractor called R. Rendall & Co. I only spent a year there, as I had a heated argument with the manager, and left to start a new job as a trainee Quantity Surveyor.

When I got to 19, my wages were six pounds two shilling and six pence a week, and that would not go up until I passed my final exams. I was getting bored with the job and wanted something more exciting and decided to join the army. Again my father's influence came to bear and after a long discussion about my future I decided to join the Metropolitan Police in London. I can still remember my father's words to this day, in a broad Devon accent, 'Doan 'e join the Army lad, cos I ain't gonna buy e out if 'e doan like it. If tis excitement 'e wants, go for the Met police in London.'

So on 10th October 1966 I joined the Metropolitan Police in London. I was put into Hendon police training school for an eight week course. At the start I hated it, I was continually being picked on by the drill sergeant for what he called shabby dress, and boots that did not come up to the same standard as the mirror like quality of his footwear. That meant early morning parade day after day.

After a week of this I lost my temper and said to the drill sergeant, 'I've had enough of this, you are continually picking on me, give me my insurance cards and I'll be off.'
'You can't do that,' he replied in a rather shocked voice.
'I can.' I answered, and turned to go and see the superintendent in charge of the training school.

The drill sergeant grabbed me by the shoulder, nearly wrenching it out of its socket, 'Hang on lad, we can sort this out, I can make sure you never have to do another parade for the whole of the time you are here.'

This sounded good, but I knew you never get anything for nothing in life and there would be some sort of catch. I turned back and looked him in the eye with suspicion, as he said, 'All you have to do is go for a little run each morning, then, while you are having a shower, all your other colleagues are on parade, and you have your breakfast at your leisure.

It sounded too good to be true, and it was. What he did not tell me until later in the day was I also had to do circuit training in the afternoon, between classes, and boxing training in the evening. It turned out I had volunteered for the training school boxing team, and that I would box against the other training school boxing team at Peel House in central London, in 14 weeks' time.

Well I must admit I wasn't too disappointed, and I did enjoy my 8 weeks at Hendon training school, and I was fitter than I had ever been in my life. I won my fight and was awarded an alarm clock by the then commissioner of police, Sir Joseph Simpson. Unfortunately this later got broken during an argument with my first wife, when she threw it at me and I ducked, resulting in it smashing on the wall.

I was posted to Holborn police station, which had a variety of areas in London to police, from Kings Cross to Charing Cross Road and from Russell Square to Hatton Garden. While serving at this police station I carried on boxing in my spare time for two more years.

After five years on the beat I transferred to traffic division. I enjoyed 6 years in this department, riding fast motorcycles and driving fast cars, but soon got disenchanted after seeing several of my colleagues killed and injured, whilst performing traffic duties.

My eyes were now looking toward the River Thames and I was thinking of joining Thames Division. I was getting older and more experienced in the police force and did not want to end up killed or injured chasing after motorists for some minor misdemeanour, as had happened to colleagues in the past. I had messed about in boats as a boy and it appealed to me to be able to do it as a policeman.

There are many stories I could go on about when I was patrolling on the River Thames, but this book is about the Underwater Search Unit, true stories that have happened in the 13 years I served there. In most of the stories only first names have been used, unless they have told me they don't mind being identified using their last name. Characters are true to life and instances are as accurate as I can remember. Some stories will make you laugh, some will make you cry, and others will make you shudder with horror. My police diver's logbook was also my diary, so please forgive me if at times it sounds a bit formal.

1983 The Beginning

About November 1983, applications were put out on Thames Division, the marine side of the Metropolitan Police, for volunteers to apply for posts as divers in the Underwater Search Unit. This appealed to me, as I had spent a lot of time diving in Malta and the thought of doing something I enjoyed in my leisure time and being paid for it seemed too good to be true.

Before being selected for the Underwater Search Unit all applicants had to undergo a few tests. One of the tests was to swim 20 lengths of a standard size swimming pool, then do the same with a weight belt and snorkel. Each applicant was then taught basic lifeline signals and how the self-contained breathing apparatus (scuba) worked. Once we were happy with the scuba, we were in turn put under the water in a blacked out mask, this was to see if anyone suffered from claustrophobia.

After all these tests were successfully carried out to the satisfaction of the Underwater Search Unit Inspector, it was then up to one's performance at an interview in front of Senior Officers of Thames Division, including the Inspector in charge of the USU, who would question the candidates as to their suitability. Most of the questions were about diving, for example, how do you feel about going underwater in nil visibility, and finding a dead body; do you understand the risk involved; what does your wife think of it; are you prepared to be on 24 hour call, and turn out at any time night or day whatever the weather.

The only unusual question I remember quite clearly was put to me by the Inspector in charge of the USU who said, 'Are you prepared to take your turn in cleaning out the porta loo on the USU lorry?' Well, I thought, of course, the unit spends 50% of it's time diving in shit anyway, so what's the big deal about cleaning the porta loo.

When the final choice was made I came second, and the reason given to me was the man that was chosen above me had previously been a Port of London diver and already held a commercial diver's certificate, and it was thought he would be more likely to pass the 8-week course at the National Police Diver Training School. So my heart sank and I thought my chance had gone.

I was already 36, and that was considered to be the maximum age for entry into the unit. The diving unit was a very small team of men out of the thirty thousand members of the Metropolitan Police Force. Entry was mostly filling dead men's shoes, by the time there was going to be another vacancy I would be over the age limit.

Anyway what happened was, the person selected was told to go to Edgware Hospital for an X-Ray. He duly turned up at the Hospital, and was told to sit in the waiting room and was puzzled as to why the man next to him was acting rather strangely. When the nurse came up to him and asked his name, he told her, and explained he was going to be a police diver. She smiled at him and said, 'Of course you are my dear.'

I think it was then he realised he was in a Hospital for the mentally retarded!

Anyway to cut a long story short, he eventually found the right Edgware Hospital, but failed the diving medical due to a high blood pressure. This was my lucky day. I was next in line for entry into the unit. I successfully passed my medical and in January 1984 joined the small team of divers that make up the Metropolitan Police Underwater Search Unit

The Metropolitan Police Underwater Search Unit 1989

Some members of the unit have asked not to be identified so I have only used First names

Trapped under a safe

13ᵀᴴ June 1984

I had been at the National Police Diving School based in Sunderland. for some weeks now, and we were starting to use more equipment underwater.

Today, 13th June, was to train us to lift heavy objects by using two types of lifting bags. One type was an enclosed air bag that was taken underwater in a deflated state to the object to be lifted.

Once the strop or chains were secured to the object by the diver, he would then surface and swim clear of the area where the lifting bag would surface. Air would then be pumped into the lifting bag via a tube from the surface connected to either air tanks or a compressor, and provided the object was not too heavy it would come to the surface to be towed ashore for recovery. If the object was too heavy the diver would simply attach another air bag.

The other type of airbag we would be using was an open airbag, it was used in the same way as the enclosed airbag, except the diver would use his breathing air to slowly inflate the airbag by putting air into the open end of it. The difference here was the diver would come up with the airbag, which gave more control in the speed of ascent to the surface.

We arrived at South Dock Sunderland about 9-30am, and began to unload the diving lorry. We were all briefed that there were two safes at the bottom of the dock and our exercise today would be to attach the two kinds of lifting bags to the two different safes, and lift them to the surface. The depth of the dock was about 8 metres, and visibility when we started was 1 metre.

We all took it in turn to carry out the exercise and at completion, the lifting bag was deflated and the safe sank to the bottom of the dock, ready for the next diver to carry out the lifting operation. The more the exercise was carried out, with the safes hitting the silt and stirring it up at the bottom, the less visibility there was.

I entered the water to do my open lifting bag operation at 11am. The first thing to do was release the ratchet handle that tightened the strop around the safe. The strop was a little stiff and required a lot of effort to free it. Once free, it was taken to the surface to start the operation, which was to take it down to the safe, put the strop around the safe, tighten the ratchet handle, then inflate the airbag, using the air being exhaled from your breathing valve.

Visibility was virtually nil, and at this point most of my operation had to be done by feel. I must have put just a little too much air in the lifting bag, as when it started to ascend, it shot to the surface at quite a fast speed. At least the safe was still attached. Previous divers had not put the strop on tight enough and the safe came off on its way up. Pleased with the operation using the open air bag I moved onto the enclosed airbag.

At 11:47 I went down to remove the strop that was on the safe used for the enclosed airbag exercise. This was a larger safe, measuring about two metres high by a metre and a half square. When I got to the bottom and located the safe the visibility was so bad I could not even see my air contents gauge. I felt my way around the safe and found the strop ratchet handle. I pulled on the release lever and nothing happened. I tried again but it was not moving at all. To get some real purchase on the handle I put my feet up on the safe and pulled as hard as I could, but unbeknown to me, as I could not see, the safe was falling towards the dock bottom, and the next thing I knew, the safe was on top of my right arm, trapping me underwater.

I tried to pull it free several times but it was useless, and now I was beginning to breathe heavily, using up more air. I was just about to call the surface when they called me, 'What's taking you so long?'
'I've got my arm trapped under the safe,' I replied.
'Don't panic, keep calm, preserve your air,' they said in what appeared a panicked voice.

Then, 'how much air have you got left?'

'I don't know the visibility down here is nil, and I'm now lying in the silt.'

Again in a panicked voice they replied. 'Ok keep calm we are going to send the standby diver down with an airline and diving valve so you will have air from the surface till we free you.'

I lay there in the darkness thinking to myself, how long would it take for the standby diver to get to me, what if I run out of air before he gets to me. I know, I thought, I'll panic. With that thought, I managed to get my diving knife out of its scabbard and started digging furiously around my arm, and at the same time pulling for all I was worth. A couple of times I cut my dry suit and could feel the cold water seeping in. Eventually, with another pull, using my feet against the side of the safe, I pulled my arm clear.

I immediately hit my suit inflation button and shot to the surface, coming out the water like a submarines missile. Now there was no air coming from my breathing valve, and I quickly removed my full face mask to get some air. I could see the shock on the faces of the instructors standing on the dockside, shouting, 'pull him in, pull him in.'

I looked over to the dock steps and the standby diver was just going down to the water's edge. My thought now was, would he have got to me in time, and if I had not panicked would I have had enough air left for him to reach me and supply surface air? On reflection I think I made the right decision at the end of the day and left my fate to myself.

When I got back to the dockside, I explained what had happened and was examined to see if I needed to have medical treatment. I said, 'I'm ok but I'm afraid I damaged, the dry suit.'

In a broad Geordie accent one of the instructor replied, 'Wye I man don't worry about that we've got plenty more, but there's only one of you.'

This was me in my dry suit going out to dive in the cold North Sea. The suit ended up with many patches and when the cold North Sea came flooding in you really know about it.

We all laughed about it afterwards, making jokes about what could have been. It was only when I got back to my room at the end of the day, delayed shock set in. I sat on the edge of my bed in the police section house, thinking about it and started to shake.

There was a knock on the door. It was one of the lads in our training team. 'Bloody hell man you're shaking, are you alright?'
I replied, 'nothing a few whiskeys won't fix.'
'Right, I'm getting the rest of the lads and we're going on the town.'

We all went down to Sunderland town centre and they kept buying me drinks, so much so I could not remember much about getting back to the police section house. The following morning I felt fine, apart from a sore head.

When we got to the diving school the instructors asked if I was ok to dive. I replied, 'well if you fall off a horse they say you should get right back on it, so let's go diving.'

I completed my police diver training after eight weeks, coming top of my class, and received my HSE commercial diver's licence that included added qualifications on recovery and preservation of evidence.

The diving students, my closest friend then from Essex Police Force, was Steve Taylor, shown sitting down. He was killed along with another police diver a few years later in a police diving accident.

Then from left to right, Paul Cook, Gary, John Botham and myself in overalls, as I had an ear infection and could not dive.

At the back the students. At the front the Instructors

On our way to a diving location in the North Sea, wearing survival suits

Headless Body

11th February 1986

On a cold February morning the underwater search unit were hoping they could have a maintenance day, but that was not to be. No sooner had we sat down for a cup of tea, the phone rang in Phil's office. Phil came from his office into our mess room with a piece of paper in his hand and a smile on his face.

'Ok,' he said, 'we have a body floating in the River Lee in North London, near a pub called Cooks Ferry Inn, Edmonton.' Everyone quickly finished their tea and put on some warm clothing. All the necessary equipment was already on the diving lorry and we set off through the snow.

On arrival at Cooks Ferry Inn, we were met by the landlord of the pub and Edmonton C.I.D. We could see there was what looked like a body floating in the middle of the River and appeared to have its head underwater.

I was top of the list this day and so that meant I would have to go in and recover the body.

Not all of our work involves going under the water; in very shallow water something as large as a body can be felt with the feet, and through experience you know when you have touched it and what it feels like. In a large area like a lake or pond, up to six of us would walk in line to cover the area more quickly, feeling with our feet. On other occasions where there is only one to two feet of water, and where small objects such as guns or knives needed to be found, we would use snorkels.

I entered the water in my dry suit, having put a little air in it to keep me afloat. Attached to my harness was a lifeline that would enable my attendant to pull me back once I had got hold of the body.

As I swam towards the body I started to smell it, and having spent 5 years on the boats in Thames division, I had pulled out many floating bodies, some so rotten that when you go to pull them alongside their limb comes off. The smell is something you never forget, and stays with you for days, you can almost taste it.

Initially a body sinks in water, and it's only when the internal organs begin to rot and fill the body cavities with foul smelling gasses it floats to the surface. The time of year, and the temperature of the water will decide how quickly the body will decay, and bring it to the surface. So this body being thrown in during the winter could have lain on the bottom of the river for up to two or three weeks.

As I got to the body, its shoulders were facing me, and I saw this hole in the middle. I felt sick, as I realized it had no head and I was looking straight down its oesophagus.

I grabbed the arm of the body and shouted to my attendant to pull me back to the bank. When we got the body onto the bank and laid it onto a body sheet one of the C.I.D. officers said, 'oh shit, not another murder investigation, we have four on the go at the moment.' The other C.I.D officer on scene turned away from the body and was physically sick.

After writing a statement, we all returned to the diving lorry for a warm cup of tea, as it was freezing.

The following day we retuned to the River Lee to search for the head. As I had not gone underwater the previous day, I was still top of the list, Dick was number two diver, so it was decided we would dive separate areas and work towards each other.

The River Lee was now covered in thick ice, and we had to break a hole for entry. This was done by continually dropping a 56lb weight onto the ice until there was a hole large enough for Dick and me to enter the water. The water temperature was checked, and it registered one degree centigrade. The air temperature was minus ten degrees centigrade. Phil, who was supervisor that day said, 'When you can't feel your hands any more, come out because you'll be wasting your time.'

I entered the water through the ice hole at 11:10am and descended to the bottom. Visibility was about one foot- good for the River Lee on the muddy bottom. As I settled down to start my search for the head, I looked up and saw my bubbles making patterns underneath the ice. This was the first time I had dived under ice and it was very exciting.

As the search went on without finding the head, the excitement soon diminished as my hands began to sting with the cold. I carried on my search until the stinging went and I could no longer feel my hands. I surfaced at 11:55am, having done 45 minutes underwater.

To my surprise on surfacing, there was a television crew on the riverbank, and a camera in my face as I took my mask off. An interviewee started firing question at me, 'What's it like down there, are you cold, did you find anything?' This was the first time I had encountered the media at a dive, but something I soon got used to.

Because this was a murder investigation I had to be very careful with my replies, and just remained very non-committal to any loaded question from the press.

In December 2011 I went on a cruise with my wife Kay, for a month on board Queen Mary 2, sailing from Southampton UK to New York, then to the Caribbean, back to New York and Southampton.

Whilst having a drink in Queen's grill lounge, I met Shaw Taylor who used to present a television programme called Police Five. He mentioned he once interviewed a police diver who was diving under ice in the River Lee, looking for a head. I smiled and said, 'That police diver was me, Shaw.' After that the stories just kept coming and we became firm friends.

Myself and Shaw Taylor in Queen's Grill Lounge Bar, on Queen Mary 2

Once dressed and back in the warmth of the diving lorry, feeling began to return to my hands, they stung like hell for ages until they just felt nice and warm. This was police diving, if I wanted to stay in the unit I had to get used to it. We could not choose when or where we dived, we just had to get on with it, or leave.

The body had a distinctive tattoo on one of its arms and was eventually identified from the tattoo. The C.I.D arrested someone for the murder and he gave a statement saying he had hidden the head in a bag in a derelict building.

Gun Found in Regents Park Canal

23rd April 1986

We were told there was a VIP visiting the American Ambassador's residents in Regents Park, and were asked to do a security search in Regents Canal near a bridge. We arrived at the canal and set up two jackstay search lines going from bank to bank across the canal. A Jackstay search consist of a rope placed on the bottom of the canal, stretched from one bank to another and held down by a 56lb weight each end of the rope.

The diver starts at one end, holding the line with one hand and searching with the other until he reaches the other end of the line. He then moves the weight and line one arm's length towards the direction he is working and continues back to the start point. When he reaches the start point he will then move that weight and rope an arm's length toward the direction the search is going. We have always found this type of search very successful, especially in nil visibility. I entered the water to carry out my search at 12:00pm and surfaced at 1pm.

The biggest problem in diving the canal is boat traffic, apart from the occasional shopping trolley, broken glass and the fear of getting a hypodermic needle used by a drug addict stuck in your hand. Signs are out out indicating diving is in progress in the canal, but very few canal users see them, and some even think they can carry on because the diver is underneath their craft, and not likely to come to any harm.

Sound travels underwater 4 times faster than in air, roughly 1500 metres per second and you can hear a craft coming from quite a distance away. The trouble is you cannot tell from what direction. When you hear the sound it plays on your mind, and you start thinking, has the lookout told the boat to stop? If you are in a shallow canal, you are always wondering about the depth of the keel of the boat coming towards you. One of the team is always posted on the bank to shout at boat owners to stop, and then the diver is taken out of the water to allow the craft to pass before diving resumes.

On my search I found hundreds of post office pre-pay telephone cards but nothing else. It turned out they were stolen in a post office raid a month previous.

The post office had a record of the card numbers and deactivated the cards before they could be used, so the robbers then dumped them in the canal.

Jim was next diver in the canal and started his search where I left off. It was only about half an hour, before he came up with a sealed plastic bag that showed something wrapped in brown greaseproof paper. Because of the importance of the security set up by police there was a mobile command centre not far from where we were diving, and we were asked to take anything we found to them.

After we completed diving the area we were asked to search, we took the plastic bag to the mobile control centre, where they put on rubber gloves and slowly opened the plastic bag. Then the greaseproof paper was pealed back to reveal an automatic gun, with a fully loaded magazine. We were later told the C.I.A, having little faith in the U.K. security services planted the gun in the canal to see how good our search techniques were.
I hope they were suitably embarrassed or impressed.

Merlin

1987

We were all sitting in the Underwater Search Unit mess room at Wapping Police station and today would be a maintenance day if we did not receive a call out. At about 10am the telephone rang, Phil answered, and asked for two volunteers who were animal lovers. Huggy and I said we would come with him to the Regents canal, Canal Road just off Mile End Road.

We drove to the location to see a very wet police rider and his horse named Merlin in the middle of the canal. Apparently the policeman was riding his horse, called Merlin, along the towpath of the canal when some workmen on the other side dropped a sheet of corrugated iron. The noise spooked Merlin and he leapt into the canal. There was no way to walk him out, the banks were too steep.

We contacted the London Fire Brigade and asked if they had anything to lift him out. Fortunately they were one of the few brigades in the country that had a straight lift, and within 10 minutes they were on scene.

The next problem was to get a harness on the horse and this is where we came in. Phil turned to Huggy and me saying, 'well you said you were animal lovers, who's going to volunteer to go in and put the harness on?' Huggy and I said both of us were not very good with horses, so Phil decided he would have to be the one to go in the water and put the harness on Merlin. We helped him on with his dry suit, attached a lifeline to his harness, and then Phil climbed down a ladder into the canal, taking with him the harness supplied by the fire brigade. When Phil got to Merlin he said, 'Hello Merlin, magic your way out of this one.'

Phil attaching the harness to Merlin

The fire brigade then shouted instructions to Phil on how to put the harness on. Once the harness was attached Merlin was unceremoniously lifted onto the towpath and re-united with his rider. His rider talked to him and examined him to make sure there were no injuries. We helped Phil out of the canal and he seemed very bemused saying, 'Well that's a first. I'm glad he didn't panic and kick me.'

The police rider wearing fireman's clothing is re-united with his horse Merlin

You just never know what sort of job you are going to get assigned to each day and that is what makes it all the more exciting being a diver in the Metropolitan Police.

Mark Peers R.I.P

15th Feb 1989.

On Wednesday 15th February 1989, Smoothy, Biffo, Jim and I were asked to take Mark Peers out on a Training Dive exercise for the day. Mark had previously been selected for a place in the underwater search unit back in June 1988, and was awaiting a vacancy.

It was decided that we would take him to Luxborough Lake, in Chigwell Essex, which is a lake that is one stage up from a swimming pool, as the water is clear, the bank slopes gently away from O to 12 feet deep, and is ideal to get Mark used to the way the diving unit works. I had dived Luxborough Lake on many previous occasions, not only as a police diver but also as a sports diver with the British Sub Aqua Club. Although none of us here on this day had dived with Mark before, we were aware he had been out with the diving unit on previous occasions, and had stated on his application for the unit he had been a member of the Metropolitan Police BSAC branch.

We climbed into the diving lorry. Jim and Smoothy sat in the front, and Mark, Biffo and I got into the passenger section of the lorry. As we drove to Luxborough Lake, both Biffo and I chatted with Mark about diving, and it appeared Mark could not wait to get into the Underwater Search Unit. Biffo had served with Mark at Waterloo Pier Thames Police station prior to joining the USU and was therefore a close friend. I had only socialized with Mark on a few occasions, and knew his wife Bernadette, as I had taken a Royal Yachting Association, Yacht Masters course with her. Mark was commenting on how he had recently just come into a small inheritance, and was thinking of going to Australia to live in the future.

We arrived at Luxborough Lake at about 9:55am, and reported to the water bailiff. We informed him of the area in the lake we intended to dive. The weather was overcast, and the lake was calm. There were a few fishermen, but well away from the area we were diving, and there were no boating activities on the lake.

After looking at our diving list it was found Smoothy was top, and therefore would act standby diver for Mark. Jim was appointed dive supervisor, and Biffo and I attendants. Mark was briefed as to what he was required to do, and was then dressed in a dry suit and checked by Biffo, who made him fully aware of where his weight belt release pin was, his air reserve, and his suit inflation, and made him physically use them to make sure there was no mistake should he encounter a problem.

He was then asked if he knew the basic lifeline signals, and was asked to repeat them. This he did very well, and

I told him that if there was no answer on a signal being given on the second occasion, it would be treated as an emergency, and I would pull him out immediately. Mark appeared quite relaxed with the equipment and we were surprised to see he even crouched down to vent his suit prior to entry into the water, which is something most experienced dry suit divers would do. His air contents were noted and recorded at 200 Bar, which at the depth he would be diving would last him more than an hour.

A jackstay search line had been set out from the shore. Mark slowly disappeared under the water, and we watched his bubbles as he went out along the jackstay. After each run he came out of the water waist deep, I asked if he was well and he nodded his head indicating all was well, this happened for 25 minutes. He then gave me five bells on the lifeline, which indicated he had found something. I returned the signal to let him know I had received it. I then gave him a signal to return to the surface which he answered to show he had received my signal.

Mark returned to the surface and told us he had found a car. We asked what colour it was. He said rusty and lying on its roof. Jim, Smoothy and I were qualified dive supervisors, and between us discussed whether it would be safe to allow Mark to actually do some easy underwater work as he had done so well on the search pattern exercise.

It was decided it would be a simple task to allow Mark to attach a rope to the axle of the car. We knew it was on its roof and there was no need for Mark to get in or under the car. It was just a simple case of following his shot line back to the car, standing alongside it and tying a bowline knot around the wheel axle. Mark was asked whether he felt confident enough to go back and tie a bowline on the axle of the car and come straight back to the surface.
He said, quite indignant, 'Of course, I am a Yacht Master as well as a Thames man you know.'

I think he felt quite hurt that we should ask whether he was competent at tying such a rudimentary knot to the car, but we had to be sure, because it would be underwater.

Mark's air contents were noted again, and his gauge was showing there were about 80 bars left which would give him 30 minutes underwater at the depth he was diving. Biffo replaced Mark's face mask, and handed him the salvage line. Mark then grabbed hold of the search line with his other hand and disappeared underwater with the salvage line following him.

I watched his bubbles go towards the car and eventually stop at the area he had previously signalled he had found the car. His bubbles came to the surface at regular intervals, indicating he was breathing normally. His bubbles then came away from the vehicle and stopped. I pulled once on his lifeline to see if he was alright. There was no reply, but the bubbles from his equipment were still coming up at regular intervals so I was not too concerned.

I informed Jim there was no response to the signal I gave Mark, and I though from the way the lifeline felt when I pulled he may be snagged and trying to clear it. Jim then said, 'Try him again, he should have cleared it by now.'

I pulled one more time, but still there was no response. Jim was now a bit concerned Mark was not answering his lifeline signals, and immediately turned to Smoothy and said, 'I think you better go down and sort him out Smooth.'
Smoothy entered the water immediately, and as he disappeared under the water, following Mark's lifeline down where we could see he may be.

We suddenly noticed Mark's bubbles change from normal to an eruption of air, consistent with a valve free flowing. Smoothy's Bubbles came closer to where Mark was, I felt the life line clear, I pulled on it as hard as I could, assisted by Jim. At the same time Biffo pulled Smoothy back to the surface. It seemed like seconds before we had Mark out the water, but as he appeared on the surface, we saw he did not have his mask on. His face was blue, and he did not appear to be breathing.

Jim and Biffo immediately started mouth-to-mouth resuscitation and cardiac massage procedure. I ran to the diving van and called for urgent assistance and an ambulance, giving location and the fact that there was a possible drowning.

I then went back to the others who were still administering mouth-to-mouth and cardiac to Mark. Between us we kept the resuscitation going until the ambulance arrived, and at one stage we thought he was coming around, but kept getting hampered with the yellow mucus and blood flowing out of his mouth and nose. We were having to continually unblock his airway.

We did at one stage use a Brook's airway, and the resuscitator that is always on site at any dive, but discarded this in favour of mouth to mouth, as this appeared to give a better chest extension. The ambulance arrived some 20 minutes later, and Mark was put on a stretcher and taken to the ambulance, while Biffo continued to give mouth to mouth resuscitation.

Meanwhile, although suffering from the trauma of the incident, we started to assess what had happened, remembering our training as police divers, and what should be done in the event of a possible fatal incident.

In training for this kind of situation it's easy, but when the real thing happens to one of your own it is very hard to concentrate and put all the emotion aside.

First we got all Mark's equipment together, listed it, examined it and sealed it into a plastic bag. This was later submitted to the Royal Naval Research Establishment at Alverstoke, Hampshire, where Mr Ian Himmens, a government scientist, examined it.

The local duty officer, an Inspector then turned up and asked if there was anything we needed? We replied no, were just sealing the diving scuba in a plastic bag.

Dave, our sergeant that day then arrived with Inspector Whitworth from Wapping Thames police station and said, 'I am sorry lads, Mark's been pronounced dead at Whips Cross Hospital, I'll drive you all to Barkingside Police Station.'

We were all absolutely shattered now, and I'm sure suffering from a certain amount of stress, but what was to come next was even more stressful. No sooner had we got into Barkingside Police Station, we were separated and put into interview rooms by detectives, and each one of us told to make a full statement concerning the incident. We all did this without any problem, but I objected to being treated as if we were to blame for Mark's death after spending 20 minutes trying to resuscitate him, only to be told at the end of it all he had died.

After making the statement I was told to go to the canteen and sit with the others, but halfway up the stairs I met Bernadette, Mark's wife, I did not know what to say, she cried and put her head on my shoulder and said, 'Oh Mac I don't blame you, I know you did all you could, but I don't know how I'm going to live without him.'

It did make me feel a little better, knowing Bernadette did not blame us for his death.

I joined the others in the canteen. We were numb and did not speak to each other for some time.

That night when I got home to the boat Kay and I were living on at the time, all I wanted to do was sit and say nothing. Kay said. 'Speak to me, tell me all about it, it's not your fault.'
I replied in an angry voice, 'leave me alone, I can deal with this on my own, go back to your mum for a while.' She got angry with me and told me she was not going anywhere, and that she would be staying with me through this awful time.

We opened a bottle of whiskey and talked, to be honest it helped, in the past I had always dealt with stressful situations on my own, my previous wife never wanted to know about the bad times I had in the police force. Kay was a different personality entirely.

The following day we all met at work and started to discuss the dive. and the why Mark died, wondering just what had gone wrong. Biffo had gone sick with stress caused by Mark's death. Apparently he found it hard to come to terms with the fact Mark had actually died, and he was given a sedative at the hospital, plus a large brandy to calm him down.

A week later we were asked if we wanted counselling. We thought a bit late for that, and the three of us, Jim, Smoothy and I, thought we could sort it out by talking amongst ourselves, but Biffo did attended counselling and said it helped.

Although I thought I was coping with the situation quite well, according to my girlfriend Kay (now my second wife) I was behaving rather strangely. We got through it though, by talk and a lot of alcohol. All we had to do now was to wait for the inquest.

 Meanwhile a Force Funeral was being arranged for Mark, and on Thursday 23rd February 1989 it was held at Croydon Parish Church. I stood in line in full uniform with the rest of my colleagues and watched as Mark's coffin passed by. I felt people were staring at us at the funeral, blaming us for Mark's death, but we knew we'd done nothing wrong and everything possible to bring him back.

Some time after the funeral, we were advised to take up legal representation for the inquest. We could not see any reason to do this, as we had nothing to hide, and thought it would look as if we had if we had a solicitor acting on our behalf, but when we heard Bernadette was suing the Commissioner of Police for negligence, we had no real option but to be represented.

There was an inquest into Mark's death and we all had to give evidence to the coroner. The post mortem results just said death by drowning, but I feel there must be some other underlying reason for Mark's death. Now we will never know.

We were cleared of any blame for Mark's death by the coroner and praised for our courage in the face of personal loss. Bernadette put in a claim for one million pounds, claiming we were negligent in the supervision of Mark's dive. She lost the claim and we heard later that she went to live in Australia.

The Marchioness Disaster

20TH August 1989

At approximately 01:46 hrs on 20 August 1989, the passenger launch Marchioness and the aggregate dredger Bowbelle, both bound downstream, collided in the River Thames just upstream of Cannon Street Railway Bridge. As a result the Marchioness sank.

A search and rescue operation was swiftly mounted under the control of the Thames Division, Metropolitan Police, but despite this 51 of those on board Marchioness lost their lives. There were 80 survivors, the majority of whom were picked up by Police launches, or by the launch MV Hurlingham, which was in the immediate vicinity.

The Skipper of the Marchioness was among those lost and, without his evidence, it was impossible to reconstruct exactly the circumstances of the collision.

What was clear however, was that although it was a fine moonlit night and in both vessels the wheelhouse was properly manned (and in Bowbelle two seamen were posted forward), neither vessel was aware of the other until it was too late to take effective avoiding action. This was the main cause of the collision.

In each vessel the maintenance of a good look-out was seriously hampered as a result of poor design. Visibility from the wheelhouse was seriously restricted and in neither vessel were sufficient steps taken to overcome this difficulty. A further major contributory factor to the collision was the failure of Marchioness to keep to the starboard side of the channel. This is linked to the failure of look-out, in that her Skipper plainly thought that the channel was clear. This failure in look-out (especially in Bowbelle who, as the overtaking vessel, had the overriding duty to keep clear), the design faults and the failure of Marchioness to keep to Starboard, contributed to the disaster.

All this stems, in part, from bad practices which have grown up over many years. Some consideration of the responsibility for these practices is addressed later in the Report but more important than who was at fault, is the vital need for remedy.

THE Marchioness is lifted after Port of London Authority divers and the police Underwater Search Unit placed cables around her hull

The Marchioness after she was lifted and placed on the foreshore, ready to be searched by police

Marchioness

Port of Registry: London

Official Number: 147526

Gross Tonnage: 46.19

Length: 85.5 feet (26.06 metres)

Built: 1923, at Oxford

Engine: Extensive conversion took place in 1979 and 1981.

6 cylinder Thorneycroft Compression Ignition

Owner: Tidal Cruises Limited Lambeth Pier, Albert Embankment, London SEI

The vessel is a Class V passenger launch operating within smooth water limits on the River Thames. She held a Passenger Certificate issued by the Department of Transport for 149 passengers plus 2 crew above Greenwich, and for 80 passengers plus 2 crew between Greenwich and Gravesend.

The Marchioness as she was before her sinking

The Bowbelle unloading her cargo of gravel as

As my wife Kay and I passed her in our boat 'Camyak'

Bowbelle

Port of Registry: London

Owner: East Coast Aggregates

Official Number: 306078

Gross Tonnage: : 1880 tons

Length: 262.2 feet (79.9 l metres)

Beam: 44.4 feet (13.53 metres)

Deadweight: 1474.92

Built: 1964, at Troon

Engine: 8 cylinder Diesel developing 137 1 KW, and giving a service speed of 11.75 knots

Owner: East Coast Aggregates

Manager: South Coast Shipping Company Limited

Canute Chambers

Canute Road

Southampton SO1 IAB

The vessel was an aggregates suction dredger.

The Bowbelle left the Metro Greenham Aggregates berth at Nine Elms at 1:12am on 20th August, bound for the Shipwash dredging grounds. She was in ballast, drawing approximately 2.0 metres forward and 3.2 metres aft and therefore, trimmed some 1.2 metres by the stern.

The Master, 31 years old Douglas Henderson, holding a Class 1 (Master Mariner) Certificate of Competency which he gained in October 1988, had been appointed to Bowbelle as his first command in May 1989. He had served with East Coast Aggregates' dredgers since 1987 and had considerable experience of Thames navigation.

The ship carried a total complement of nine, including two deck officers besides the Master, who was well rested, having had the previous night in port and also having slept in the afternoon.

The Marchioness left Charing Cross Pier at a time not precisely recorded but probably about 1:25am. The skipper, Stephen Faldow, was a licensed Waterman and well experienced on the river. The only other full time crew member was the Mate, aged 21, who was an apprentice Waterman. There were also 2 bar staff and a number of passengers estimated by the Mate (who survived the accident) at 110. There was, however, no actual count made and the true number was substantially more, and appears to have been 127, giving a total complement of 131.

She had been chartered by a photography agent, Jonathan Phang to celebrate the 26th birthday of Antonio de Vasconcellos who was a charismatic young financier. The passengers were their guests, many of them in their 20s, some friends and others working in the fashion industry. The planned cruise, for which (as is common on night-time river cruises) a disco had been provided as part of the entertainment, would have taken Marchioness down river as far as the Tower of London, then back to Charing Cross pier to land some of the passengers. It then travelled down river again to Greenwich returning to Charing Cross pier at about 5:45 am.

The Marchioness (with the same Skipper and Mate) had already completed an evening cruise between 7pm and 9:45pm on 19 August. It has not been possible to establish how much rest the skipper had had before that, but he had been off duty for at least 15 hours.

The weather was fine with a full moon and good visibility. The moon was on the starboard bow to both vessels as they headed down river. There was a flood tide, and high water at London Bridge was 4:48am.

Bowbelle reported to Thames Navigation Service (Woolwich Radio) at 1:13am that she was singling up ready to depart. She reported again when she was at Vauxhall Bridge at 1:20am and Waterloo Bridge 1:35am. For the benefit of other river users Woolwich radio included her as being outward bound 'through bridges' in the routine half-hourly information broadcasts at 1:15am and 1:45am. This was normal practice. No broadcasts were made by or concerning Marchioness, which was also normal.

Both vessels passed through the centre arch of Blackfriars Bridge. Above Southwark Bridge, the Marchioness overtook another cruise boat, the Hurlingham (also on a night-time disco cruise), and soon afterwards Hurlingham was also overtaken by Bowbelle.

In the latter vessel the Master was conning the vessel and the Second Mate was steering. (It is customary for the officer of the watch to steer during the passage through the bridges, under the supervision of the Master, but largely using his own judgment.) Both officers on the Bowbelle held Thames Pilotage Exemption Certificates.

The Chief Engineer was also on the Bridge, the Third Engineer was on watch in the engine room, and two seamen were on the fo'c'sle. One seaman was the lookout and the other was standing by to raise the mast once the vessel was clear of Tower Bridge. The engine was at half ahead and the ship was making good a speed of about five knots.

The Marchioness was being conned and steered by the Skipper, and at about this time he was joined by the Mate. The Marchioness speed appears to have been no more than about 3 knots.

Both vessels passed through the centre arch of Southwark Bridge and shaped up to pass through the centre of Cannon Street Railway Bridge, about 125 metres down stream. Before they reached that Bridge, at about 1:46am, the collision occurred.

In the Bowbelle, the two seamen on the fo'c'sle had first noticed Marchioness at about the time of the passage through Southwark Bridge, which is less than a minute before impact. They were emphatic that when they saw the boat she was some 3 points on the starboard bow, about 45 metres off and apparently on a parallel course and, therefore, about to be overtaken; the passing would be close but not unusually so for the river. They sensed no danger and made no report to the wheelhouse. This was in accordance with their normal practice of only reporting when a hazard was perceived.

It would appear from their evidence that Marchioness then altered to port so as to converge. They attempted to shout a warning, which was heard by a few passengers on the deck of the Marchioness, but not in either vessel's wheelhouse. Perhaps because of the noise of the disco which was in progress on the boat, the warnings went unheard. The noise from the disco was commented on by witnesses ashore.

In the Marchioness, shortly after she passed Southwark Bridge, the Mate, who was standing half in and half out of the wheelhouse, looked aft over the port quarter and saw the dredger very close. He shouted a warning and thinks that the Skipper put the throttle full ahead. (It was found at full ahead when the vessel was raised). The fact that he saw Bowbelle over the port quarter tends to support the evidence that the vessels were converging, although he also said that Marchioness 'appeared to be shaping up for the central arch of Cannon Street Bridge in a normal way', which would suggest a less marked convergence than the Bowbelle statements imply. The

Mate was, however, unable to be positive about the course the Skipper was following.

No one in Bowbelle's wheelhouse saw Marchioness at all before the collision.

There is a slight bend in the river, and the centre arches of Southwark Bridge and the next two bridges downstream of Cannon Street and London Bridge, are not quite in alignment. Both vessels therefore needed to alter course a little to port after clearing Southwark Bridge. However, to make it easier to line up for Cannon Street and London Bridges, Bowbelle initially and as she began to emerge from Southwark Bridge, made a small alteration to starboard.

Looking upstream to Cannon Street railway bridge, scene of the collision between the Bowbelle and the Marchioness. You can clearly see the bridge arches are not in line with each other.

If the Marchioness came to port at the same time, this would account at least in part for the courses converging, though there were probably other factors. As the vessels closed on each other, the angle of convergence was much increased, and the Marchioness came athwart Bowbelle's bow. There was heavy impact abaft amidships on Marchioness's port side, which rolled her over to starboard beyond her beam end.

Damage extended from the deck to well past the keel, showing that Bowbelle virtually pushed the smaller craft under. She continued to pivot on the bow, and passed down Bowbelle's port side, floating on her side, but water must have been flooding in freely throughout her length through all her deck openings. One of the surviving bar staff recalls that Bowbelle's anchor 'came in through the window' of the upper saloon.

When the Marchioness was raised, this saloon, which was a superstructure of very light construction, was found to have been completely torn away, probably by the anchor. (This was fortunate for those within.)

The Marchioness floated on her side long enough for the Mate, who had been thrown into the water, to clamber on to her port side and open a door which led into the dance deck, allowing some passengers inside to escape. She then sank, having drifted to a position about 183 metres East of Southwark Bridge and from the North Bank.

With a strong flood tide this implies that she would have sunk within about a minute of the collision.

The alarm was raised by a vhf call timed at 1:46am from the MV Hurlingham, and a search and rescue operation was very quickly mounted, under the control of the Thames River Police. This operation involved numerous craft augmented by helicopters but despite their efforts there was a heavy loss of life. Because there was no record of passenger numbers, uncertainty remained as to the number lost for some considerable time; but it has been established that the correct figure is 51. There were eighty survivors, mainly because the roof of the upper deck was torn off, spilling people into the river.

The force of the impact caused the Bowbelle to lose control, and she struck successively first the southern pier of the central arch of Cannon Street Bridge, and then the northern pier. She sustained some damage but there were no injuries to those on board.

The wreck of Marchioness was located and recovered later on 20 August, and bodies were found in the wreck, the remaining 27 being recovered from the river. The upper saloon was recovered separately, from a position nearby by the police underwater search unit.

This was how it happened according the Marine Accident Investigation Branch of The Department of

Transport. Now to how the underwater search unit and I were involved.

It was 19th August and my partner Kay, my brother Bruce and I had just completed a week's holiday cruising on our boat and home, 'Camyak'. The trip had gone without incident apart from the fact we nearly sank when coming into Ramsgate harbour. This was remedied after beaching the boat and a repair of the U section of the exhaust, lasting two days and costing over one thousand pounds.

We were now cruising up the River Thames to our moorings at Brentford Marina. As we passed Tower Pier we noticed the Marchioness was moored alongside the pier, letting off passengers. As we continued on up river under Cannon Street Railway Bridge and Southwark Bridge we remarked on what a nice day it was. On passing Metro Greenham Aggregate berth at Nine Elms Reach, we saw the Bowbelle alongside, and from the plimsole line it appeared she had unloaded all her cargo of gravel.

As we continued towards Brentford Marina it got dark and we could see quite clearly with the full moon shining on the river. When we got to Brentford Marina, there was not enough water to get through the locks, it now being low water. It was decided to moor alongside a barge in the middle of the river, get some sleep and enter the lock in the morning.

Sometime during the night there was a beeping noise, and Kay shook me and said, 'what's that noise?' I replied, half asleep, 'Oh maybe I left the alarm on.' And turned over and went back to sleep. Unbeknown to me it was my pager, and the control room at Wapping police station were trying to get hold of me because of the disaster.

We woke early and entered the lock to Brentford Marina, only to be met by the harbour master shouting, 'They have been calling for you, they want you at Wapping as soon as possible, there has been a boat sunk near Cannon Street Railway Bridge. I moored the boat alongside the pontoon and waved Kay and Bruce goodbye and drove to Wapping. As I approached Wapping, I could hear helicopters overhead.

Outside the police station were many vehicles, some from the Royal Navy, Ambulances, Air Sea Rescue and others. I had to drive a long way past the police station to park, then walked back. As I entered the police station it was full of people, so I gathered all my diving gear together and walked through the station yard that was at that time being used as a temporary mortuary. Bodies were being labelled and photographed.

I was ferried up to the scene of the collision between the Bowbelle and the Marchioness, and transferred myself and my diving gear to the police boat being used by the rest of the team. Also there were the Port of London Authority divers (PLA), ready to attach cables to the Marchioness to lift her. But before that, we had to carry out a procedure of knocking on the hull to see if anyone was alive inside. To facilitate an extended diving time in the tidal water, they closed the Thames Barrier, stopping the tide coming in and giving us a larger window in which to dive.

We liaised with the PLA divers who were more used to dealing with engineering diving and it was decided we would assist with the attachment of cables around the hull under their supervisor. This done, the cables were then slowly raised by a PLA crane barge called the Hookness. Once the Marchioness hit the surface, the weight was greater, and raising had to be halted to allow the water to drain from her. The Marchioness was then taken to the north shore where she was secured, awaiting the next low water. When she was finally sitting on the shore at low water the Thames Barrier was kept closed until all the bodies were removed.

The first day was a long day for us and we were looking forward to getting back to Wapping for a nice meal, we knew in this sort of situation all food would be provided by catering branch of the Metropolitan Police.

On getting back we washed our equipment down, re-pumped the air tanks in case we were required again, and then had a shower. On entering the canteen for our meal, we were told there was nothing left; they had given our meals to the Royal Navy divers. We were gutted and I said, 'well where are the Navy divers?'

The canteen manager explained they, along with everyone else, had gone home. The only thing she could do for us was a sandwich. We were not a very happy bunch of divers.

They had called Air Sea Rescue, Royal Naval divers, and many other organisations to assist in the operation, but in the end the only people that could do anything were Thames Division, their divers, the PLA divers and salvage men. We searched for a few more weeks in the area of the collision, and recovered many bits of the Marchioness, the biggest being the roof.

The disaster was found by the Marine Accident Investigation Branch to have been caused by the poor visibility from each ship's wheelhouse, the fact that both vessels were using the centre of the river, and the lack of clear instructions to the lookout at the bow of the Bowbelle.

In 1991, the skipper of the Bowbelle, Douglas Henderson, was tried for failing to keep a proper lookout, but after two juries were deadlocked he was formally acquitted.

A Coroner's Inquest on 7 April 1995 found the victims had been unlawfully killed.

Following pressure from the Marchioness Action Group, whose publicity front had been handled by photographer and party attendee Ian Philpott on 14 February 2000, John Prescott, as Secretary of State for the Environment, Transport and the Regions, ordered a formal investigation into the circumstances of the collision, to be chaired by Lord Justice Clarke. Lord Clarke's report also blamed poor lookouts on both vessels for the collision, and criticised the owners and managers of both vessels for failing to properly instruct and monitor their crews.

In 2001 an inquiry into the competency and behaviour of Captain Henderson by the Maritime and Coastguard Agency concluded that he should be allowed to keep his master's certificate as he met all the service and medical fitness requirements. However, they "strongly deprecated" his conduct in drinking 5 pints of lager in the afternoon prior to the accident and for his admission that he had forged some signatures on certificates and testimonials in order to obtain his master mariner certificate of competency in 1988.

Subsequent to recommendations made in the Clarke report to improve river safety, the Government asked the Maritime and Coastguard Agency, the Port of London Authority and the Royal National Lifeboat Institution (R.N.L.I) to work together to set up a dedicated Search and Rescue service for the tidal River Thames. Consequently, on 2 January 2002, the R.N.L.I set up four lifeboat stations at Gravesend, Tower Pier, Chiswick and Teddington.

The Bowbelle was herself lost seven years after the disaster. Having been sold to the Madeira dredging company and renamed Bom Rei, she split in half and sank on 25 March 1996 off the Coast of Ponta do Sol, Madeira. The Tubarao Madeira Diving Organisation discovered the wreck 6 months after it sank. The wreck is still in good condition and offers refuge to a varied range of fish and marine life. After only a short time, marine plants grew in abundance on the wreck and the boat has become a pulling point for divers.

A memorial to the victims can be found in the nave of Southwark Cathedral, not far from the site of the disaster, where every year a service of remembrance is held for those who lost their lives.

Body in Hampstead Pond

Friday 3rd August 1990.

It was just after 8 o'clock in the evening. I was relaxing on our boat, which was moored at Brentford Marina, just outside London, on the banks of the River Thames. Kay had cooked a lovely meal that evening, but that's not unusual for Kay, she is the perfect cook, and with limited space living on a boat, has to be very inventive. One Christmas day she did a whole Christmas meal including a 10lb turkey in a wok.

We had finished eating and were just finishing our second bottle of wine. We were thinking of making a night of it and starting on the whiskey, as tomorrow was the weekend and no work. The phone rang. We looked at each other, hoping it was not a call out for me. Unfortunately it was, and I could see the disappointment in Kay's face.

The reserve officer at Wapping police station said, 'Sorry Mac, it's a call out to a body in Hampstead Lower Pond'.

Hampstead Lower Pond is not as it sounds, and bears more resemblance to a lake in size. Hampstead is a suburb of London and a very nice place to live. It has a large common with several ponds. Some of the ponds are for fishing and there is one where you can swim.

'Ok,' I replied, 'I'll be there as soon as possible.' I did not really feel like it, having eaten to bursting point.

I rolled off the back of the boat and climbed into my car, a Toyota Land Cruiser, and drove as fast as was legally possible to Wapping. When I arrived at Wapping I found they had only been able to get four other members of the diving team and our civilian driver Tony. Phil, who was in charge, was there and Mick, Brian and John arrived later. Although five is enough to carry out a dive, we always like to have as many Unit members as possible on call out for the simple reason we do not know what we are going to encounter when we get there, and too many hands are better than not enough.

The diving lorry was checked to see we had all the equipment needed to carry out our diving operation then all the members present got into the back of the lorry and we set off. We drove direct to Hampstead Ponds where we were met by the local duty officer who explained that most of the witnesses had now gone home, but there was a police constable who was there at the time, and who they could get hold of if necessary. He had worked from 6am to 2pm that day, and had now gone home.

The information we got was that apparently the man had drowned some six hours before we were called out. He had been seen to walk into the lake then disappear under the water. One member of the public dived in to try and save him but got into trouble himself, and had to be rescued.

 Then Hampstead Heath Park keepers, who were also in attendance, had said one of their men was a diver and could get his diving equipment and try to recover the man. That proved no good because as soon as he entered the water he found there was no visibility and ended up totally disorientated. So eventually, and as usual, they decided the services of the Underwater Search Unit were required.

I could see Phil was furious, and we were not all that pleased either, as it was getting dark and things always look different in the dark. Distances are harder to estimate and witnesses seem to get the position wrong.

The policeman who we were told had witnessed the drowning arrived, and it turned out he had not seen the incident, but was told by other people who had seen the man drown where and when he had last been seen on the surface. He pointed to an area in the lake, where he thought the man was last seen. As he was doing this a little voice said, 'No mista, it weren't there.' in a strong cockney accent.

Two little boys who had watched us arrive, had been at the scene when the incident happened, and could give us first hand information. The boys pointed to a location yards away from where we were first shown. The boys also knew how to get there. They led us through a path that went through a clump of trees and bushes.

It was pitch black and we had to use torches to illuminate the area. I was on the diving list as number one diver, and Brian was my standby. Neither of us relished the thought of diving for this body, but I was first in and Brian hoped, as I did it, would not take long to find it. The worst part when recovering a body is the searching. The longer it goes on the more your imagination plays tricks on you.

I started my search by slowly going down the search line into the dark, dirty pond water. I could feel the bottom of the pond consisted of thick mud, leaves and twigs. Visibility was absolutely nil, and the use of a torch would have been pointless because of the high density of silt in the water, so it was a 'feely' job, just using hands and legs.

As I completed my third run along the search line I began to think, 'this is going to go on for some time'. Then suddenly, there was a tap on my shoulder. I jumped with fright. It really did feel like someone tapping on my shoulder, and the old imagination was working overtime, playing tricks on me again. What had happened was, I had trodden on a branch that went from one of the trees around the pond into the water, and as it sprung back it hit my shoulder.

I slowed down my breathing to calm down and said to myself, 'don't be so stupid, it's only a dead body'. Just as I was thinking that, I touched what felt like a nose and mouth. I jumped again, pulling my hand away quickly, and then slowly putting it out again to confirm what I felt was the face of a person. Yes this was the body.

I signalled five bells on the life line to let them know I had found the body, by pulling my lifeline with one hand five times. I then checked over the body by running my hands all over it to feel whether there was anything sticking out of this person. This was standard procedure so you could answer any questions at the coroner's court at a later date. The last thing to do was to remember which way the body was lying in relation to the shot line, to determine its position.

Having done everything required for future evidence, I put my arms around the waist of the body and signalled on my lifeline to my attendant to pull me in. I felt the lifeline tighten, and I was on my way to the surface assisted by my attendants pulling the lifeline and me. On reaching the surface I was helped, with the body, onto the bank where we laid it onto a white body sheet.

The drowned person was a man. He was in his late twenties and quite small in build. There were no marks on the body, and so we were happy to leave it in the hands of the police constable.
'Well that's our job over,' said Phil, rubbing his hands, 'It's down to you now son,' looking at a young, very shocked looking Policeman.

We left the young policeman to arrange for the police surgeon to come and declare the man dead and to remove the body.

All our muddy diving gear was then taken back to the lorry, and before putting it away, we sprayed it down with metasan, a strong disinfectant. Brian and I changed out of our diving suits and drank a well-earned cup of coffee.

The only thing left for me to do now, before I went home to my boat, was to write a statement giving the circumstances of how I found the body, and what the water was like. No visibility, no current, and the bottom clear of obstruction.

I arrived back on my boat at 1:30am in the morning. Kay was awake, and asked me all about the search. We sat for about an hour drinking a large whisky, and then climbed into our bunk and fell fast asleep.

You never stop learning in this job, and one thing I learnt on this occasion was, Believe nothing of what you hear and only half of what you see.

The Water Take off Tower.

19th August 1991

It was about 17:30pm on a summer evening. Kay and I were relaxing on the aft deck of our boat drinking cool gin and tonics when the phone rang. It was Wapping Police Station. They explained that an eight year old boy was seen to fall into the water at Lockwood Reservoir, which is in Forest Road, Walthamstow, North London.

Apparently the child had been climbing around the lip of a water take-off tower, which was situated on the edge of the reservoir, slipped and fell in, then disappeared under the water. A water take-off tower is where they draw off water from the reservoir to process it into drinking water.

As I had been drinking, I arranged for a local police car to take me to Wapping. I arrived and started to get my diving equipment ready. Dave, our sergeant, arrived and told me he had managed to get five other members of the diving team to come, which made seven divers in all, plus Tony our driver. The divers were Brian, Dick, John, Biffo, Chris, Dave and me. We looked at the diving list and saw that Dick was top of the list, and so was first in the water and I was number two diver.

None of us really like looking for bodies, especially children, and I was pleased Dick was first in and hoped we would find the boy quickly. Because of the serious nature of the call, and the fact that the parents were on scene waiting for something constructive to be done, we arranged for a Traffic Division car to give us a blue light escort to Lockwood reservoir. We arrived within half an hour of leaving Wapping, which was good going for that distance in London.

On arrival we were met by three other Thames Division Officers who had gone there prior to the Diving Unit being called, to see if there was anything they could do.

Thames Water officials who own the reservoir were also there and stated that at the time of the accident, the pumps in the tower were working and they were drawing off water from the reservoir into the tower. They confirmed they had now turned off the pump and closed all valves.

Dave asked whether there were any grills over the water take-off tube on bottom of the tower. The Thames Water officials did not know but thought not. Dave then asked if they had any plans of the water tower. They said they had, but would have to send for them, and did so immediately. Again Dave asked, to make absolutely sure, if all of the valves relating to the water tower had been turned off and screwed down tightly. He was told that it's all done electronically now, and if the light shows, its shut. We accepted that.

Having to dive near water sluices and valves is very dangerous, as it only needs a slight gap in the valve to cause suction and trap a diver against it, and the deeper the water, the greater the suction.

Dave decided that we would first search around the outside of the water tower. Dick and I quickly got changed into our diving suits, while the rest of the team started to make up the scuba sets and take all the diving equipment up the bank of the reservoir to the water take-off tower. Light was now fading as Dick entered the water and started his search around the water tower where the boy had last been seen.

As his search continued, he got near to a bell-mouthed opening which was about three feet in diameter, and drew water off the reservoir. He kept close to the wall of the tower and placed his hand in front of the hole to see if there was any flow of water that may have dragged the boy into the tower. It was OK, so he went in about eight feet but found nothing. Dick then continued searching.

After 40 minutes he had covered a large area around the tower and found nothing. It was now thought the boy must have been sucked into the tower through the three foot bell-mouthed intake tube, and then to some point unknown into the pumping system within the tower.

The plans were now given to us by the Water Board officials. They showed four different levels, each with its own hatch cover allowing access to each compartment via an enclosed ladder, and going down to a total depth of 80 feet to a further tunnel, which then led to the filter beds. The water board had no idea whether there would be sections of the platforms missing or whether the valves were fully closed, as it had not been inspected for a long time.

The platforms on each level were made up of cast iron gratings split into 4 separate segments, making a total area of 10 feet in diameter. Each platform had its own entrance hatch 2 feet square, which opened onto an enclosed ladder going down to the next level. If the hatch or floor just below the take-off port was intact it was just possible the boy might be in that section of the tower.

To get to this chamber meant negotiating a three no surface dive. That means if anything went terribly wrong with the diver's equipment and he had to surface immediately, he could not do so without first negotiating the three enclosed ladders that led to each trap door before he reached the surface, which would not only take up more time but also add to the danger of getting his equipment or life and communication line caught in the process.

Dave looked at me with a sad expression and said, 'Well kid, you're next on the list so it's up to you. I don't mind if you don't want to do it as you know and I know there is an element of danger involved, but then that means I'll have to go in, because I'm next on the list, and I'm not too happy about that.'
The only other option was to drain the reservoir down to empty the tower and we were told that would take two or three days.

I did not relish this dive but I thought I couldn't let the side down now. I also knew the parents of the boy were at the scene and it would not be nice for them to go home and think about their boy inside that cold, wet water tower, even if he was dead. I said to David I would do the dive provided there was a standby diver on the second level of the tower, and one to assist me should an emergency occur, and two to help feed my life line and communication line through the hatches and ladders so there was less chance of me getting tangled up in the enclosed ladders.
Dave said, 'yes I planned to do that anyway.'
He would also have Brian standing by on the first level in his diving gear.

I entered the water at 8:25pm with a torch to examine the second level; this was seventeen feet six inches from the first level and was reached by climbing through a small hatch and going down an enclosed ladder. I could only assume they only climb these ladders when the tower is completely drained.

When on the second level I attempted to open the next two foot square hatch leading to the third level. It was rusted shut, and nothing I did could shift it. I surfaced and asked for a crowbar to wrench the hatch open. After a lot of effort, and beating my valve with the exertion, this failed. I called on my underwater communication for a rope to be lowered down to tie to the hatch so that the lads on the surface could try and pull it open.

When I had finished tying the rope through the grills on the hatch, I stood clear and said, 'right start pulling.'

At first nothing happened so they pulled again. Suddenly I saw the floor move. They had pulled out one of the four floor segments instead, and the hatch was still rusted shut. I told them to stop, before the segment fell through to the next level. When the silt and rust particles had settled enough for me to see, I took another look.

They had pulled it out just enough for me to squeeze through a gap to the enclosed ladder leading to the third level.

Dick, who was now under the water with me, helped push the heavy cast iron segment to a safe position, so that it didn't fall through on top of me while I was below that section. I then started my descent into the third level. The water was now very murky due to the rust and silt that had been disturbed by our attempt to open the hatch.

On reaching the third level I started going around the sides of the tower, feeling my way across the cast iron grating that made up the floor, I had about 8 inches of visibility. I suddenly came face to face with the boy. I could see in the murk he was laying face down on the grating, his head pointing away from the intake hole. Rigor mortis had already set in and he was as stiff as a pole.

I swallowed with sad emotion, not something I normally do when recovering bodies, and said to myself, 'poor kid, so young to die, so much to look forward to.'
 I called the surface on the underwater communications and said, 'I've found him, lower a rope down.'
 The rope was fed down to Dick who then fed it through the opening and enclosed ladder down to me. I lifted the boy upright and looked at his face. I can still remember how peaceful it looked, no strain or anguish.

Holding him upright and against me, I tied the rope around his chest and under his arms. I called the surface team again, 'Ok, pull him up slowly.'

Dick started to pull the boy up as I guided him through the enclosed ladder rungs and through the section of cast iron floor that was now missing from the second level. The rest of the team then pulled the boy to the surface where he was examined by a doctor, and pronounced dead. There were a lot of tears from his parents before he was put into a body bag and taken away.
Dick and I surfaced, completing our dive at 9:15pm.

The depth from the first level to the third level was approximately 53 feet. However had the body gone down through to the filter beds it would have been virtually impossible to recover, it being 80 feet to the bottom of the tower, and then going through a tunnel to the filter beds. The only alternative in those circumstances would have been to drain the tower, that meant the large reservoir too, and that would have taken a very long time.

We recover a lot of bodies in our profession as police divers but I do not think any one of us ever get hardened to recovering children. I would like to think I could, but deep down inside I think it must affect the way we look at life - differently to ordinary members of the public.

Dave, being so pleased with our work, said he was going to recommend Dick and I for a commendation. We did not think for one minute it would actually happen, but a few months later Dick and I were called to Scotland Yard and presented with framed Commendations. This was the first time anyone in our unit has ever been commended for recovering a body, or for that matter anything, but I would like to think that this gesture was in recognition of the Unit's work as a whole, because without the rest of the team the diving operation would not have been possible in the first place.

I later attended the inquest into the death of the young boy. Thames Water was criticized, firstly, not having signs on the fences surrounding the reservoir warning people of the dangers, and secondly, not having a grill on the bell- mouthed intake on the tower. Not that it would have stopped the boy drowning, he would have just been found outside the tower instead of inside. The coroner was pressing for Thames Water to be prosecuted for corporate manslaughter but as far as I know this never happened.

There are now lots of signs around Lockwood reservoir and a grill has been fitted to the water- tower intake.

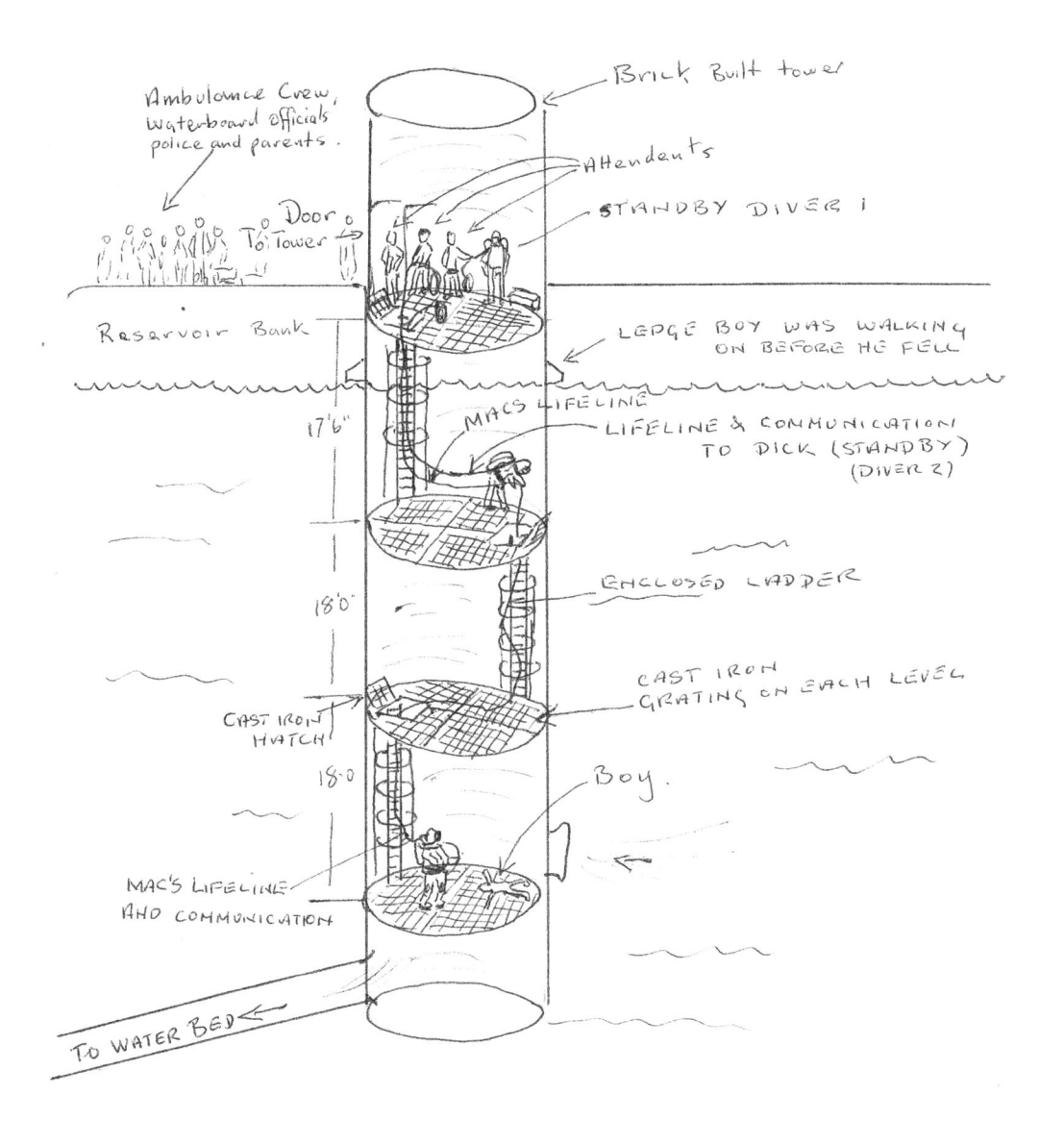

The water take-off tower that was used to draw water from the reservoir to the filter beds.

> **Commendation**
>
> On *3rd December 1991* at *Territorial Operations Headquarters New Scotland Yard.*
>
> *Constable Mackenzie Moulton*
>
> was commended by the Deputy Assistant Commissioner
>
> *for outstanding skill and ability in recovering the body of a young child who had drowned in tragic circumstances in 30' of water at Lockwood Reservoir, Walthamstow on Monday 19th August 1991.*
>
> Deputy Assistant Commissioner

The commendation I received for volunteering to carry out the dive necessary to recover the body of the boy. My colleague Richard Amas (R.I.P) who did standby diver for me received a similar commendation.

Boat child crushed under his home

2nd May 1992

On Saturday 2nd May 1992, I was lazing on the aft deck of my boat, a 45-foot Dutch Steel Motor Cruiser named 'Camyak'. Kay and I were living on it and enjoying life afloat. The phone rang and I had a sneaking suspicion it was a call out. I was right. I was told a child had gone missing at Church Wharf, Coney Road, Chiswick, West London.

Apparently the child lived with his parents on a large vessel similar to a trawler, and named 'Victory'. He had been left playing on the deck, but when the parents later went to check on him, he was nowhere to be found. After searching themselves without finding him, they called in the local police, who then mounted a search of the surrounding area. When the search proved negative, and they took into account he lived on a boat, it had to be suspected he might have fallen into the River Thames, and so our team was called out to continue the search underwater.

Phil, our Inspector, was in charge, and nearly the whole of the team turned out. When we arrived and surveyed the scene we noticed the boat was moored on the North West bank of the Thames, facing South West. The tide was now ebbing, and racing away at quite a speed. It was too dangerous to dive at this stage of the tide, and so we had to wait until low water when the tide would be slack, and safe to dive.

At 11:30pm the tide had dropped sufficiently to allow safe access for the divers. It was so low breathing apparatus was not needed, and a wade search was carried out around the boat but nothing was found. By this time the tide had turned, and we would have to wait until 4am when we knew it would be high water, allowing us to dive under the vessel.

While waiting for this we talked to the local police, and one said the father of the 4 year old boy had spoken of hearing a crunching noise through the hull of his boat as it settled on the bed of the river. This made us all feel quite sick and upset as to the condition we may find the boy in. At 4am we looked at the scene and decided it would be too dangerous to dive under the hull of the boat, and that it would probably be better to moor the vessel down river from the search area.

We retired to get some rest, and returned at 6am on Monday 4th May 1992, ready to search the area where the vessel sat on the river-bed at low water. As the tide receded we could see the indentation the boat made in the mud. With the foreshore now exposed it was like an oval pond full of muddy water. Mick, John and Jim went onto the foreshore and started a wade search of the indentation made by the boat in the mud, which was about 20 yards long and had about 18 inches of water in it.

As Mick turned on the South West point to return across the indent, and about 5 yards into the water filled hole he kicked something. He felt down with his hands and found the lower limbs of the child. Mick called to John to come and help him lift the boy up. They looked at each other with anticipation before they lifted, wandering what they were about to find. Later John said he had a vision of what he was going to see, knowing the child had been crushed under the boat as it settled on the bottom.

As they lifted the child up they were both upset at what they saw, the head was almost completely flat but had not burst, and the boy was fully clothed with one shoe missing. He was then very carefully taken up the riverbank to the shore and handed to a Police Officer assigned to the case. We all get used to dealing with bodies, but I don't think any of us get used to recovering children, and especially in tragic circumstances like this one.

We later found out that Mick was greatly affected by this, as at the time his own son was of a similar age. We did not think about the effect on our colleagues, and we all react differently to different situations. Mick was very quiet afterwards, and should have been driven home not left to ride back on his motorcycle. He said he could not remember the journey home. It was as if the motorcycle was on autopilot, and all through the night could not sleep for thinking about the boy. We all scoff at counselling for this type of thing but are now fortunately beginning to realise we are not superhuman, and it does have a place in our type of work.

Taxi Driver found in the dock

10th March 1993

On the morning of the 10th of March, 1993 the Diving Unit got a phone call at Wapping Police Station from the murder squad that had been set up to investigate the possible murder of an Asian Taxi Driver. The murder squad was working from North Woolwich Police station. The story was relayed to us was, that apparently the taxi driver's last fare was two white men who asked to go to an address in Silvertown. Silvertown is an area where the Royal Albert and Victoria Docks are situated, and at one time they were very busy with shipping from all over the world, bringing merchandise to and from the United Kingdom.

The taxi driver was a married man with children and always went home at night without fail. On this particular night he had not returned home, and his family, fearing something had happened to him, reported it to police. The police at North Woolwich police station also got an anonymous phone call giving information that the taxi driver had been murdered and was in the Royal Albert Dock, Woolwich, and was in his car.

We were asked if we would meet the murder squad detectives at the Royal Albert Docks with a view to searching for the car, a Datsun saloon, registration A192 FLR. We arrived at the Dock early in the morning and spoke to the detectives assigned to this case. The only information they had to go on was the car 'might be' in the Royal Albert Docks. What a joke that was, this dock is over a mile long and would take months to search, doing it from start to finish, so we had to look for possible signs as to where a car may have gone into the dock.

As the detectives left to carry on their enquiries we were assigned a liaison officer called Glenn. Our first task was to walk the docks, and to look for scrape marks or missing pieces of concrete on the edge of the dock, indicating a car may have gone in. We found a few and marked them in numbers with a yellow crayon, relating them to bollards along the dock edge that also had white painted numbers on them, making perfect reference points.

After this was done, our next task was to map out the dock bottom with our Eagle Fish Finder Depth Sounder. This also had a printout facility so that when something showed up on the printout that looked like a possible car we could mark it with a red pen with the number of the bollard it was nearest to. We painstakingly steered the inflatable with the depth sounder attached up and down the dock, doing three runs in all at ten feet apart, making a maximum distance of thirty feet from the dock wall. We did not think a car would go any further out than 30 feet from the dock edge. You can imagine the length of the printout after we had covered the length of the docks three times. We then stuck the three runs printed out together with sellotape to give us a complete picture of the dock bottom and marked all the lumps in the trace the size of a car, and lined them up with marks on the dock wall.

The diving team in the Royal Docks

We started diving on the first spot at the beginning of the dock, near Manor Way swing-bridge. Glenn our CID liaison officer who would be with us as long as we were diving on this case, suddenly said, 'Don't you blokes have a break?'

I replied, 'yes, shortly we will stop for a cup of tea.'

After two hours diving we stopped for tea, and Glenn said, 'What about some breakfast then, haven't you got anything on board this lorry of yours?'

'No.' I said, 'just tea or soup if you want it.'

Glenn looked most put out and said, 'I can't function without a good breakfast. I'll have to make arrangements tomorrow.'

After tea we carried on diving well into the late evening. On each blip shown on our trace we found a car, most of them old and rusty and nothing like what we were looking for.

On 11th of March 1993, we arrived back at Albert Dock to continue our search early in the morning. Glenn was there to meet us with a smile on his face. He had two large carrier bags with him. He smiled and said, 'well lads, when you're ready for breakfast, I've got it all here.'

He had brought with him eggs, bacon, butter and bread, enough to feed the whole team.

Our team today consisted of Dave our sergeant, Brian, Biffo, Chris, Smoothy, Mick and me.

We started diving, and again found more old cars, but still not the one we wanted. After three hours diving we decided to have a break for tea, this turned into breakfast as Glenn had started cooking the eggs and bacon and lots of toast, the smell was irresistible, and we all had some. We were not used to this sort of luxury, and asked if he would like to become permanently attached to the unit. We dived all day, up until we lost daylight, but still nothing.

12th March 1993, we were back at the dock again and started diving. We were just about to put another diver in the water when Glenn's mobile phone rang. We waited as he put his hand in the air, like a policeman stopping traffic, and then he said, 'I have just had information that we are diving in the wrong place, and that the car is up near Connaught Road Bridge.'

This was the complete opposite end of the dock to where we had started our search.

We marked the spot where we had finished off, and loaded the diving gear onto the lorry. We then drove up to Connaught Road Bridge and started to dive there. At the end of a long day we had found a few old cars, but still not the Datsun we were looking for. We had Saturday and Sunday off, as the murder squad could not afford to employ us over the weekend.

On Monday morning 15th March 1993, we started diving where we had left off at the Connaught Road Bridge end off the dock, and by the end of the day we were well past the area where we were told the car might be. We all had a sneaking suspicion that we had been thrown off the scent and had been given false information, possibly because someone had seen us getting near to the location of the Datsun. It was decided that tomorrow we would go back to the other end of the dock and continue on where we had left off four days previously.

We arrived early on Tuesday morning 16th March 1993 and after a quick cup of tea started diving. After diving all morning we had a short break for tea and bread rolls, the cooked breakfast idea had worn off, I think Glenn was having one before he came to meet us.

We started diving again at 14:45. Mick was next diver in the dock and this is what he said about his dive in his official police statement.

It was about 15:00; I touched what felt like a large object, I thought it was smooth and thought it had not been in the water for very long. I informed the surface on my communications. I stood up and could feel it was a vehicle. I moved to my left and around to what appeared to be a side, and could feel a free wheel around a tyre; this indicated to me that the vehicle was upside down.

I knelt down and moved left, I could feel the quarter light window and door, the window felt slightly open at the top and the door felt slightly open, but just on the catch. I pushed it closed. I continued to move left and noticed the angle of the vehicle was such that it was buried in the Dock bottom. I could feel some of the door and noticed the window was open, at the same time I felt the wing mirror in the silt. This indicated to me the car was facing the dockside or bank.

I was asked regarding my air, but could not see the contents gauge at this point. I moved back along the side of the vehicle and to the rear, checking a body's length away from the vehicle. I came to the car and stood up, standing still to allow some of the silt to settle. I felt around the rear of the vehicle and noticed it had a boot, not a hatchback. I felt the rear screen was intact. I felt the rear number plate and having ascertained where it was touched my visor to the first letter to the far right. In the dim light and silt that was now clearing I could see an upside down 'A'. I continued to move along the number plate using this method to read it, stating each letter and figure as I could read them. The number plate read 'A192 FLR'.

I was again asked about my air, I could only see the gauge needle at ten o'clock, but not the figures, giving me a possible 80 to 100 bar of air. I checked the boot was shut. I was told this was the vehicle we were looking for. I moved on top of the vehicle over the offside rear tyre and pulled my bottom line in from the south and tied on a small loop around the rear axel. I was asked to leave the vehicle and return to the surface. I arrived at the surface and completed my dive at 15:11.

On the surface we were all jumping for joy and it proved our theory that we were being watched and were given false information about the car's location. All that was left to do now was to get the vehicle out and hope the body was inside, if it wasn't, the job could go on forever, he could be anywhere.

Glenn called his office excited with the news he was about to impart. We arranged for a vehicle to come and lift the vehicle onto the dock. It required a crane that could perform a straight lift so the car was not damaged, and if the body was anywhere near the car it would not be disturbed or pushed into the mud. A firm was called and told exactly what was required.

Meanwhile, we decided to get the vehicle ready to be hooked up by attaching chains to it. Dick was the next diver on the list. He entered the water at 15:42 and started to attach the lifting chains to the rear axle. A line was then attached to the chains and then brought to the surface to keep the chains taut. Dick surfaced at 16:10

having completed this part of the operation. We now just had to sit and wait for the crane to arrive.

At about 17:00 a crane arrived but it was the wrong type. There was no way it could perform a straight lift, and there was no hydraulic extension arm to put out over the water. You can imagine the comments that came from the lads. The crane operator contacted his firm and arranged for another crane to come to the Dock.

Crane lifting a car out of Victoria Dock

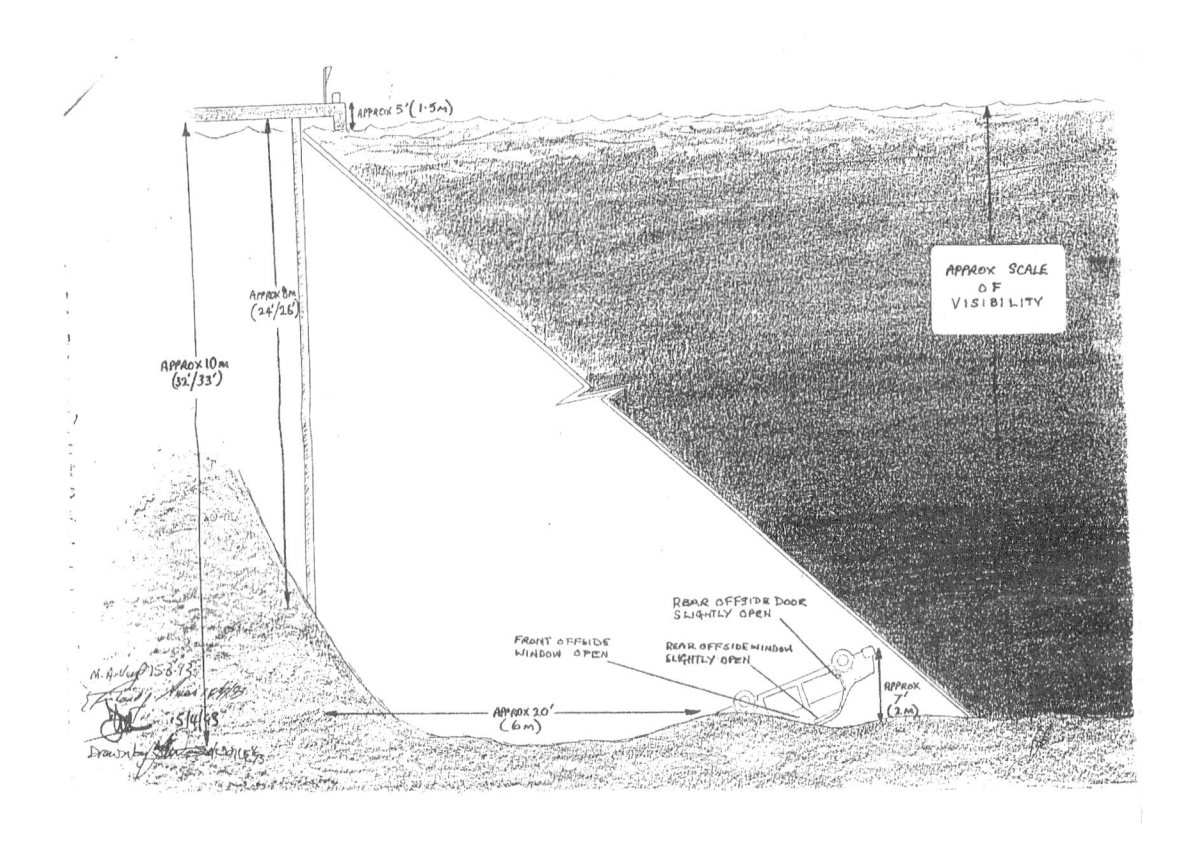

This is a copy of the sketch drawn by Mick to go with his statement, showing distances and depths and how the car was laying on the bottom of the dock

At about 19:00 the crane eventually arrived and started to set up close to the dock edge. Meanwhile Dick entered the water again to prepare to attach the chains already on the Datsun, to the crane hook. This was going to be a tricky job as it was now dark and Dick would be working in nil visibility. Information had to be relayed from Dick to the surface attendant and then to the crane driver, so that the large hook on the end of the crane cable was placed exactly in the right position to enable Dick to link it up with the chains.

Dick was kneeling on top of the bottom of the car holding a line that was attached to the hook of the crane, as the crane driver moved the hook, from the position the rope went away from Dick, he could tell where it was, and instructed the crane driver via the communications officer on the surface. It was a slow process and took some time to get the hook in the correct position. When Dick was sure it was overhead, and in the right position to link up with the chains, he asked for the hook to be lowered very slowly.

Eventually the hook was married up with the chains and Dick surfaced at 19:18. As the crane started to lift the car to the surface we waited with bated breath. The car broke the surface and the crane driver paused for a few minutes to allow the water to drain out the car, so reducing its weight. He then continued lifting it high above the water before swinging it over to the dockside. We shone our lights onto the car, hoping the body was inside.

Once the car was over the dock, it was slowly lowered down, water still pouring off it. As it came to rest on the dock, black mud fell from the car. The smell was bad, and we gathered around and peered into the car. The doors were opened and the inside examined. Nothing was found. We were very disappointed because now it meant a long search for the body. It could be anywhere, and was too small to be picked up with the echo sounder to enable us to narrow it down to a specific area in the Dock. Now the car had been found, the detectives were firmly convinced that if the car was in the dock there was a very strong possibility the body of the taxi driver was too.

As the search for the body was going to be a long operation and the CID wanted it done as quickly as possible, we decided to ask Thames Valley Underwater Search Unit if they would assist us in the search. They said they would be delighted to assist and arranged to meet us at Wapping Police Station the following day.

At 07:00 on the morning of 17th March 1993 Thames Valley Underwater Search Unit turned up at our headquarters at Wapping Police Station. We briefed them as to where we were going to search. We decided to start at the point where the car was found and each team would work in opposite directions away from that point.

When we arrived at the Royal Albert Dock we showed Thames Valley USU the point where the car was found. They were eager to get on with their dive and started to set up their search pattern straight away. This search pattern consisted of a shot line going down to a jackstay laid along the wall of the dock for about twenty-three meters. Danny, their diver, entered the water and commenced his search at about 11:20am, searching between the dock wall and the search line (jackstay).

At about 11:25, only five minutes into his search he called on his communication and said, 'I've found a body.' The first we knew about it was hearing a loud cheer from Jill, one of the few female Police divers in the country, who shouted with excitement, 'We've got it, we've got it.' We could hardly believe it but hoped it was the one we were looking for.

Danny describes his search in his official police statement as follows.

I discovered the body of the man. He was lying head first facing to the west. I searched around the body and discovered it was caught on a piece of metal jutting up from the Dock bottom, this metal was in the region on the mans hips and the body was slightly curled up in the foetal type position. The head was facing away from the dock wall.

I informed the surface. I then recovered the body and it was lifted out onto the dockside where it was handed to Detective Constable Glenn.

Danny then returned to the water to take water samples, one at the top and one from the bottom. You are probably wondering why the need for water samples. Well, in all water there are microscopic unicellular plants which exist in large numbers in all fresh and sea water. They posses an almost indestructible silica skeleton of many variations, and are called diatoms. Specific diatoms are particular to certain locations, depths and types of water. The samples taken can them be put under a microscope and matched with the water that is taken out of the lungs of the body by the pathologist. In this way it can be determined whether he drowned in the dock or was drowned elsewhere, and then thrown into the dock.

Now full of the joys of spring, and delighted that we had found the body so soon, we decided to celebrate by putting the kettle on for a cup of tea. Glenn, who was also with us, could not believe it either and eagerly got on his mobile phone to the Murder Squad. As we stood drinking tea and coffee and praising Thames Valley Underwater Search Unit for finding the taxi driver, all that was left for us to do now was wait for forensic officers, and the undertakers to arrive to take the body away.

Our job was over sooner than we expected. We thanked Thames Valley USU for their assistance and were pleased that it was them that found the body, making it all the more worth their while coming all that way.

Two men were later charged with the murder and found guilty at the Old Bailey some months later.

Ship's bottom search

14th April 1993

A large part of our work these days is assisting Customs and Excise with drug searches on, or I should say in our case, under ships.

Prior to our dive today we had a meeting with Customs and Excise officers who informed us that there were ships coming into Britain that may have torpedo type canisters bolted to the bilge keel. The bilge keel on a large ship is like a long piece of metal running nearly the whole length of the ship, welded to the hull. It is there to prevent the ship rolling. There would usually be one each side of the hull. They project anything from eighteen inches to two feet from the hull, and would be ideal for clamping contraband onto, to be later released by a diver without being seen.

The torpedo like canisters that would contain the drugs were about 2 feet in diameter and anything up to 12 feet long, and packed full of heroin. They were usually made of fibreglass and had G clamps built unto the fibreglass to enable them to be clamped onto the ship's bilge keel. The ships that they suspected were on what the Customs and Excise called 'Hot Routes' and that meant from countries like South America and Africa. The ship's cargo usually consisted of raw sugar.

Our task today was to search a ship called MV Botic which was anchored in the Thames estuary about five miles east of Sheerness, and waiting to come up the River Thames to unload its cargo of sugar at Tate and Lyle, North Woolwich.

We were due to carry out this search as a joint operation with the Essex Underwater Search Unit and arranged to meet them at Tilbury Docks. Nigel, the sergeant in charge of the Essex team gave us a briefing before we were due to set off and showed us pictures of one of the drug canisters that had been recovered on a previous search. We had the Essex Police launch to take our team and equipment to the ship and the Essex diving team followed in a large ribbed inflatable boat. We loaded the diving gear onto the boat and it was not long before we set off from Tilbury heading East towards Sheerness and the mouth of the River Thames estuary.

Shortly after leaving Tilbury it started to get foggy, and as we progressed towards the mouth of the estuary the fog got thicker and thicker until visibility was down to about 50 yards. Thank heavens for radar. We stared at the green dots on the radar, and the boat crew pointed out to us which were buoys and which were ships. It helped to get rid of that eerie feeling of not knowing where you are in the fog.

As time passed by we approached Southend pier, it was clearly shown on the radar, but could not be seen in the darkness and the fog. As we watched it disappear past us on the radar the Boat's navigator said, 'Look, you can now see the ships moored in the estuary. The one we want is about number three in the line of those dots on the radar,' pointing to the radar screen.

Chris and I who were the divers for our team were already dressed in our diving suits. We went up on deck and peered through the fog, looking for the ship. When we were about 100 yards away, we could just make out the faint glimmer of its deck lights and as we drew closer we realized how big this ship was, with its sides like a wall in front of us that stretched out into the fog.

My imagination started going wild. I thought, 'here we are in the middle of the Thames estuary, no sight of land or any other ship, in the dark and fog all around us. If they are carrying drugs and wanted to get away they could blow us out of the water and no one would be the wiser.'

I hoped the Customs and Excise were on board and had everything under control. I stood on the edge of the deck ready to jump into the water if bullets started flying. I could see Chris was doing the same and I wondered if he had the same thoughts as I had. We talked, and he admitted he was thinking exactly the same thing.

Then there was the most welcome voice on the ship's radio. Customs and Excise communicated with us and told us everything was ready for us to dive under the ship. They had an engineer in the engine room, who had made sure all intakes had been shut off and the propeller had been locked to prevent it turning.

As we secured the police launch alongside the ship that dwarfed our vessel, Phil and John climbed up the Jacob's ladder that was put down the side of the ship. Once on deck they liaised with the Customs and Excise. Essex Underwater Search Unit said they would do one side of the ship if we did the other side, and the rudder housing.

Phil and John dropped a shot line in the centre of the boat, which would enable me to go down and find the bilge keel. My scuba gear was now put on by my attendant, I placed my full face mask on and tested the valve, double checked the reserve button and contents gauge, and carrying a torch strapped to my arm, I rolled off the side of the police boat into the water and finned towards the shot line. It was now dark as well as foggy and I could only see what was in the beam of my torch.

The bilge keel of a large ship

And above the bilge keel can be seen the water intake

On reaching the jackstay I descended the side of the ship until I found the bilge keel, which was some 8 metres below the surface. It stuck out about two feet from the hull of the ship and was about four inches wide. I grabbed hold of the bilge keel and started to fin my way towards the bow of the ship. After what seemed an eternity as I was finning against the current, I finally reached the bow of the ship.

I told the surface I was now at the end of the bilge keel and had found nothing. They replied, 'ok come back to the shot line, and then start your search towards the stern.'

It was a lot easier now as I had the current with me and only had to use my fins for control. As I reached the shot line I informed the surface I was now starting my search going towards the stern. The bilge keel was a mixture of red and rust colour in the light of my torch, as well as looking for the torpedo canister I was also looking for marks that may indicate something may had been clamped on to the bilge keel previously.

As I got nearer to the stern I could hear the sound of an engine inside the ship getting louder and louder. I hoped the inlets were fully closed and that I would not get sucked into an inlet, otherwise I'd end up like a potato being drawn through a chip cutter.

Eventually I reached the end of the bilge keel, and again reported this fact and told them I had found nothing. Once more I had to fin against the strong current, and returned to the shot line and surfaced. When on the surface I was helped aboard and asked if I was alright to do standby diver for Chris, who was the next diver.
I said, 'yes I'm ok and have enough air left in my tanks for any emergency.'

We then got the Essex Police to position their boat as close to the stern as possible so that we could start our search of the rudder housing. On some big ships the rudder housing can be up to six feet in diameter and it is possible to go up into the housing where there is usually a lip large enough for something or even someone to hide there.

There was an occasion of illegal immigrants being found there in the past. The diver was doing a routine search of the rudder housing, came up from under the water into area of the housing with an airspace, shone his torch around and saw all these little faces looking back at him, they must have been as scared as the diver. Apparently when customs went on board to inspect the ship, the ship's crew unbolted the inspection hatch to the rudder housing, and told the illegal immigrants to hide there until customs had gone. They then bolted the hatch down again. The question remains, would they have unbolted the hatch if the diver had not found them?

Chris was going to do the search of the rudder housing and when he indicated he was ready to go he held onto his mask with one hand and his air bottle with the other and jumped into the water. He then had to fin a short distance towards the rudder of the ship.

His sharp Scots accent came over the communication speaker, 'reached the rudder.'

His attendant communication officer acknowledged, and then there was a short pause. 'I have found the rudder housing and I am going up inside it.'

'Ok,' replied the surface communication officer.
'I am now in the airspace inside the housing and it goes up another ten feet,' again in a strong Scots accent, then a short pause, 'there's nothing in here, returning to the surface.'

We saw Chris surface near the rudder, and then fin back to the police boat where he was helped aboard. Essex informed us they had completed their search and they had found nothing.

We do a lot of ship's bottom searches for Custom and Excise and it makes it all the more pleasant when we get a chance to dive in salt water for a change and actually get to see what we are looking for instead of feeling around in nil visibility which makes up 90% of our work.

The Customs and Excise thanked us for our help, and we sailed off into the fog, heading back to Tilbury Docks and feeling satisfied that we had done a good job, even though nothing was found on this occasion.

Body in Burgess Park and body in a box

30th May 1993.

It's Sunday 30th May 1993, and its 3:45am. I've been married for seventeen days now and life is good. I'm warm, happy and looking forward to a long, lazy Sunday, with Kay.

No such luck. Suddenly the phone rings and wakes me with a start. I think to myself as I rub the sleep out of my eyes, 'Oh no, please not this time of the morning.'
I go to answer the phone, switching off the answer phone, which has by now started to cut in.
'Hello,' I say sleepily.
'Good morning Mac,' says 'the burst mattress'. Geoff Hogg, a man who never recovered from the flower power days, and still vaguely resembles a hippy of the 60's, got this nickname because that's what his hair and beard looks like, says in a very educated voice,
'We have got a nice call out for you this morning. Some drunk decided to go for a swim in Burgess Park, and didn't make it.'
I reply with a yawn, 'ok I'll be at the station in about 15 minutes.'

I am now living in an apartment called Gun Wharf, in Wapping. It is about a 2-minute walk to the police station, and I'm always the first to arrive. Now at the police station I start to get the lights ready, making sure they all work and finding out as much as I can about the location so we know what other equipment to take. Forty minutes later seven of us are assembled at the station.

All the necessary diving gear is now on board our 14-ton purpose built Underwater Search Unit lorry, and off we go. We always use a different route each time we leave the police station so that no one can target us on a regular route. At this time in my career the threat of an attack on the Underwater Search Unit is very real. We were informed by MI5 that because we were involved in security searches to find underwater and underground bombs, we were on their list of possible targets.

We arrive at Burgess Park, which is just off the Old Kent Road, London. After setting up a search pattern and putting a diver in the lake, it wasn't long before we recovered the body and we just had to wait for the police surgeon to certify him dead.

The body of the man recovered was near a fountain, which was turned off, and a witness who was at the scene gave very good information as to where the drowning man was last seen to sink below the water.

'That's it,' I thought, 'won't be long before I am back home, and can get back to bed, cuddle up to the wife's warm bum and drain all her warmth into my body. Lovely.'

No such luck, halfway home we received a call to go to Willesden. Willesden is a suburb of London and was about a forty-minute drive from our present location. The message relayed to us was, someone had spotted a box in the canal, and it was believed there might be a body in it. The police who were now on scene thought they could see a head at the top of the box where the lid had apparently come off.

We arrived at the Grand Union canal that flowed through Willesden. The box, which was like a tea chest, but of a better construction, was clearly visible under the water. We sent a diver in to attach a rope to the box and the pulled it to the canal bank. We pulled it up onto the towpath. The box measured approximately four foot high by about three foot square and all that could be seen amongst the muck inside the box was the top of a head. The smell was bad, and it made the CID at the scene quite sick.

The box was left intact to preserve evidence and then removed to the local mortuary, where apparently when it was opened, was found to contain the decomposed body of a male of between the ages of 20 to 23 years. There was a hole in his head which looked as if it had been caused by either a hammer or bar of some 1 inch in diameter. The bottom of the box was filled with concrete. Definitely the best suicide I've seen since Alberto Calvi hung himself from Blackfriars Bridge!!!!

We were then asked to search the immediate vicinity of the canal where the box was found, for anything that may relate to the body. Just what, we were not told, but everything had to come out, be it a gun, hammer, iron bar, or clothing, and if we came across it, the lid of the box.

On one of my searches at the location my heart jumped when I thought I had found another body. My hand slid over the slimy form of what felt like a woman's torso and head. It was stuck in the deep silt at the bottom of the canal. I thought to myself, maybe we're dealing with a serial killer here. I wondered if her guts would fall out as I pulled the torso from the mud.

I signalled five bells to the surface diver's attendant, telling him I had found something. He returned my signal. I then signalled four and five, which tells him to assist me up. I put my arm around the torso and was pulled to the surface. As the water cleared near the surface I could see the green slimy form of the object I brought up with me. I passed it up to the rest of the lads who looked quite shocked until they got hold of it and realised it was the torso of a full size female manikin that had been thrown in the canal, and from the growth of the green slime it had all over it, it had been in for some time. We all had a good laugh when we discovered it was not real and as a joke left it lying on the side of the canal in a body cover for the CID to discover.

After some time we had covered quite a large area either side of where the box was found and we were all very tired. We decided to return to Wapping Police Station where a hot shower was very welcome. I arrived home at 2:30 in the afternoon and was pleased to see Kay waiting with a welcome large scotch.

We returned to the Grand Union Canal on the 1st June, now with additional information. One, it was definitely not a suicide, and a murder investigation was set up. Two, we were looking for an object similar to a weight lifting bar that may have been used to hit the murder victim over the head, and also if we came across it, could the CID have the lid to the box.

Back in February '93 the Diving Unit was called to search a lake in Mitcham, Surrey. Prior to the search, the murder victim's car, a red BMW, was found with a wreath on it near this lake. From information received it would appear that he was somewhat of a womaniser and had women all over the country. Maybe one got jealous of the others and reaped her revenge, at this point in time we still do not know.

What is known is that he was murdered with an instrument similar to a hammer or the end of a short dumbbell bar. As he was a weightlifter, it has been said he always carried them in the boot of his car so it is more than likely this was used to murder him. There were no weights found when his car was discovered abandoned in Feb, and we had obviously been looking in the wrong place. We were asked to search lakes and ponds in the Surrey area for several weeks. This of course was between searching other locations with regard to other murders that had occurred in these weeks.

The searching of the Grand Union Canal at Steels Road, Willesden NW10 went on for 3 more weeks, but no further evidence was found.

Two men drown on a sunny day in Denham

Sunday 1st May, 1994.

It was a lovely weekend and today was the first day of May. Both Kay and I were looking forward to a very relaxing long weekend as we had Monday off work as well.

The week before, we had moved into our new home, overlooking the river Thames at Greenland Passage, near South Dock Marina, London. It was somewhere we were very familiar with, as we had lived on our boat called 'Camyak' in the marina next to our new home. We had lived on Camyak for some 5 years prior to moving to Wapping.

It was great living in Wapping, and being so close to the police station I was based at, but it would only be a few years before I retired, and we decided to sell the apartment in Wapping while prices were still high. After selling, we found a duplex apartment for rent right on the banks of the Thames and next to the marina entrance; it was the perfect way to spend the next few years in London.

After getting our new house looking nice, Kay and I decided we would retire to the bedroom for the afternoon and a well earned rest, but before that some passionate love making which always made us relax and drift away for a few hours. I was just rolling over to drift off to sleep when the phone rang, a voice on the other end said, 'Hello Mac, this is Sue.'
'Oh hello Sue,' I replied with a smile.
Kay looked at me with a puzzled expression, and replied in a loud voice so that Sue could hear, 'Who is Sue?'

I carried on my conversation with Sue, who said in a very relaxed voice, 'Would you like to come diving this afternoon, we have two men who have fallen from a boat that was on a lake in Denham, Buckinghamshire, and we require the assistance of the Underwater Search Unit?' Sue had such a nice telephone voice, one just couldn't say no.
 I replied, 'yes alright Sue, I will be there in about half an hour.'

On arrival at Wapping Police Station at 3pm, I went straight into the C.A.D room and asked Sue the full extent of the incident and who in our team she had so far managed to call out. She gave me a print out of the incident, and it showed me the location was Savay Lake, Moorhall Road, Denham Buckinghamshire, and explained that a boat had sunk, and that four men were in the boat. Two had got safely ashore but two others were seen to go under the water and not surface, that was at 14:33pm

It also showed the world was there, London Fire Brigade, the Ambulance Service, the local Police, Traffic Division, the flying doctor from the London Hospital, the local emergency doctor, Air Sea Rescue from Manston and of course the press. As always we were the last to be called, and this has always been an annoying part about this type of incident, as all the other services can do nothing until we get the poor persons concerned to the surface, but like most areas of the police service at this present time, cost seems to be more important than life. If they can save money by not calling us out, they will, and so we are left to be called out as a last possible resort.

On this occasion we managed to get six members of our team to come out. Myself, Bob our sergeant, now in charge of the Unit, John, Mick and Chris, and our New driver Graham, now nicknamed 'The Sirocco Kid', because of a small accident he had a few days earlier, where he cut through the side of a VW Sirocco that was parked on the side of the road, opening its panels like a sardine tin. It was caused by one of the lockers on the side of the lorry flying open as he drove down Wapping High Street.

Soon, some of the others who had been called out started to arrive at Wapping Police Station. We started to load everything we thought we would need onto the lorry. Lights, lifting bags, depth sounder, body bags etc, and as it was a large lake we decided to take the inflatable dinghies with us and hitched them onto the tow bar at the rear of the lorry. After about 45 minutes the last two team members, Bob and Mick arrived.

I had already arranged a police escort to Denham as we only had Blue Lights on the lorry and for some unknown reason when they fitted them they refused to fit warning sirens. As we sped along the streets of London, with blue lights and headlight flashing, our police car escort in front of us did the same but had its warning sirens screaming away. As we approached red traffic lights, cars would stop for the police car but for some crazy reason totally ignored our blue light and blocked our way by trying to drive across the back of the police car. This was so frustrating and caused the driver of our lorry to use a few naughty words. It took another 40 minutes to get to Denham, even with the escort.

On arrival at the lake we liaised with the local duty officer, an Inspector, and the Fire Brigade's equivalent ranking officer. The Fire Brigade already had two boats on the lake searching around the general area the men were last seen. Fortunately they had pinpointed the sunken boat, which was going to save us time setting up our Echo sounder on our inflatable.

When the boat, which we now discovered was a fibreglass flat bottom punt about 12 feet long sank, there were two lines attached to it with fenders on the end and they were now floating on the surface above the sunken punt. To save time launching our boat, the fire brigade volunteered the use of their new Dory type craft as a platform for our diving operation. Their boat also had the facility where the side of the bulwark could be taken away like a door, giving direct access to the lake at water level.

We loaded the diving gear into the fire brigade boat and set off to the centre of the lake. On this dive Chris was supervisor, Bob and John were the divers and Mick and I were the diver's attendants.

We arrived to where the fenders were floating above the punt and started to lay a jackstay search from where the punt was, but parallel with the bank and extending some considerable way either side of where the men were last seen. John was first in and started the search, I think we were all hoping it would not be too long before he found the bodies, but after 50 minutes he was asked to check his air and John indicated he had 100 bar left. It was decided to get John out, and with the 100 Bar he had left he could do a standby for Bob. Bob entered the water and as he did so we thought that they couldn't be far away now, so it wouldn't be long. Every time Bob stopped to examine something, we thought yes, he has found it, but no. Bob came out after over an hour in the water.

It was getting cold now and none of the surface team had dressed for a prolonged search into the evening. The sun disappeared behind the trees and I started to get goose pimples, I also had wet feet as water had come in from the opening in the gunnels when each diver had pulled himself on board.

It was decided that we were close enough to the bank now to lay a search pattern from there. Also it was now dark, and lights would be easier to set up on the bank. I signalled to the Sirocco Kid, who was watching us from the bank that we had finished. He knew exactly what to do, get the tea ready and put the heater on in the lorry!

We had a short break and talked to Dr Gareth, the Flying Doctor from the London Hospital. We asked how long it took him to get to the scene, he said 8 minutes. We told him it took us 40 minutes with a police escort. We discussed the fact that in this type of incident there was nothing he could do until we arrived to get the men concerned to the surface. He agreed, and said we should meet some time and see if in future cases where there is the slightest chance of saving someone, we may have the use of the London Hospital Helicopter to transport divers to the scene. I'll believe it when it happens!

The fire brigade had now set up some good lights on the bank where we were to continue diving. The next two divers in were Mick and me. Chris was still supervising and decided as time was marching on to put both Mick and I in at the same time, working on two jackstays about 15 metres apart and 18 metres out from the bank towards the centre of the lake. I entered the water at 9:17pm and Mick a minute after me.

As I descended down my jackstay I could see a faint blur of the lights above the water, then it got blacker and blacker until I could not even see my air contents gauge. I felt my heart beating fast and concentrated on regulating my breathing to slow it down. At the same time I was saying to myself, I hope I find them soon I don't fancy an hour of this.

As I reached the end of my jackstay I could feel the weight securing it to the lake bed, and by this time I was comfortably settled and just waiting to bump into one or maybe both bodies. As I swung my body around the weight, getting ready to move it a body length, my feet kicked something large and solid.

I knew the feel. Having searched in nil visibility for many years you get to know what things are by feel, just

like a blind man. I felt my heart beat increase; it had to be a body. I pulled the weight toward it, and then started to feel around. First I could feel the arms and hands, then I went down the torso to the legs and then back up again to the head. I called to the surface (we now had vocal communication with the surface), 'I've found one!'
'What?' they replied in a stunned voice.
I repeated, 'I've found one of the bodies.'
'Already?' was the reply, 'Do you need assistance?'
'Wait.' I replied.

I then ran my hands over the body to see it was intact, that there were no knives sticking out of it and there was nothing around the immediate vicinity that may be related to the body. I did feel that he was wearing glasses, and made sure they were secure. Once I was satisfied that everything was in order, I put my arms around his chest and asked my attendant to pull me towards the bank.

I could see a faint light on the surface and knew I was getting near the bank. Once at the bank I assisted the others to get the man ashore. Dr Gareth examined the body and pronounced life extinct. I then re-entered the water and continued the search for number two victim. I continued my search for another 15 minutes, and then heard over the underwater communications Mick say those lovely words, 'I've found the second body.'

I know this may sound a bit strange but to have recovered the bodies after such a long and difficult search made us all feel elated. Had we not found them after Mick and I dived, we would all have been too tired to carry on safely and would have had to continue the following day. When that happens I always feel so sorry for the relatives, knowing their loved one is still in there in the cold murky lake.

After stripping off and packing away the diving gear, which was now thick with mud and smelt terrible, our next priority was to get to the nearest pub for a well earned drink before they closed. We pulled up outside one just up the road from the lake and piled in just as they were calling last orders. I think the staff knew who we were, all dressed in navy blues and covered in mud. The landlord looked at us and smiled, saying, 'Don't worry lads you did a good job tonight. We don't mind pulling a pint for you before we close.'
The beer went down in a flash and took away the taste and smell of the lake.

We were all very tired by the time we got back to Wapping Police Station, but we still had to wash down the diving gear and have a hot shower. It was now 1am and we had been working for 12 hours non- stop, and were wanted back the following day, or should I say later the same day, to recover the punt as it was required at

Hounslow Police Station to be photographed for the coroner.

We decided we would start the next day at 7 am so at least we could enjoy some of the Bank Holiday with our families. Now that I had to get home for some sleep, public transport had stopped and I had no private transport, but fortunately I now lived right on the river's edge next to Greenland Pier, and the night duty boat crew kindly volunteered to run me home in a police boat. I arrived home and Kay was still up. She cannot sleep when I'm on a call out.

I told her I was going to jump into a hot bath to relax myself before going to bed. I slid into the hot steaming water, and then was greeted by Kay with a large glass of whisky in her hand. She knows my weaknesses and likes so well. When I had finished soaking in the bath she told me she had some hot food for me downstairs if I was hungry? I'm always hungry! What a diamond she is. My previous wife would have been fast asleep in bed, and no way would want to hear about my diving operation.

When I could not eat any more I hit the sack, and as soon as my head touched the pillow I was fast asleep. It only seemed like seconds before my childish alarm clock was sounding to the sound of a horse galloping and neighing, telling me there was another hard day's work ahead.

I arrived late at Wapping. The lads who lived a long way from the station had stayed there, and slept on the floor. They were already loading up our diving lorry and putting the dingy onto the towing bar. I felt guilty (but not too guilty!) for being late.

Just before we left for Denham I telephoned my younger brother Bruce, who lives only a few hundred yards from where we would be diving. I told him the story and that we would be diving there again today, and maybe we could meet after the dive. It's not very often we get the chance to see each other these days and it was an ideal opportunity.

We arrived at the lake again, unloaded the lorry, got the outboard onto the Zodiac inflatable and launched it into the lake. As Mick was the last diver in, he now assumed the role of supervisor. Chris and John were the divers and Bob and I were attendants for the divers.

Once we located the punt, Chris entered the water and dived down to the bows to attach a lifting bag. Shortly after, John entered the water and dived down onto the stern to attach two lifting bags, and at the same time made sure the engine was secure and was not likely to drop off. John then came to the surface while Chris was left to inflate all the air bags.

Before long all three of the yellow lifting bags could be seen on the surface and it had lifted the punt off the bottom of the lake just enough for us to be able to tow it to the shore. This had to be done very slowly as there was a lot of weight involved and going too fast tended to make the punt sheer off either side of the Zodiac.

Once near the shore where it was shallow, John and Chris started to bail out the punt to make it easier to tow back to our trailer. This done, we then started to tow it back to where we originally launched our Zodiac. As I steered the inflatable towards the shore I could see my brother had turned up, it was nice to see him after so long. I knew there would be a lot of catching up to be done, and lots more to talk about since we last met.

The punt was man handled and dragged ashore, It was very heavy, and before we could lift it onto the trailer we had to remove some very heavy boards that had been placed on the bottom of the punt, then under that was a lot of shingle which was also removed. Once the punt was on the trailer and secured ready to take to Uxbridge Police station, Bob suggested I stay with our Zodiac until they returned. This was a good idea on Bob's part as it gave me plenty of time for Bruce and me to talk.

As we sat talking, friends of the two men who had drowned the day previous stood looking towards the spot in the lake where they were last seen. It was remarked what good men they were, and how one who was a swimmer went back to help the other who was a non-swimmer, resulting in both losing their life.

Their other concern now was what was going to happen to those in charge of the fishing club, as all four men in the punt were not wearing life jackets, and as far as I was concerned the punt was not in very good condition. I could only reply to them that it would be a matter for the coroner to decide, and sympathised with them on the loss of their two friends in tragic circumstances.

Time flew by and before I knew it I was waving goodbye to my brother Bruce, and on my way back to Wapping. All that was left to do now was for Mick and I to make statements about our recovery, and later attend coroner's court.

Security search for HRH the Duke of York

Thursday 19th May 1994.

Security searches are now quite a large part of the Underwater Search Unit's workload, and today our job was to search the West India Dock wall, and bottom of the dock 3 metres out from the wall, prior to the arrival of three Royal Navy minesweepers, which were going to moor in the dock. One of the minesweepers was called HMS Cottesmore, the other two HMS Atherstone, and HMS Hurworth, and a Canadian ship named HMCS Toronto. HMS Cottesmore was Captained by His Royal Highness the Duke of York, hence the step up in the security operation

HMS 'Cottesmore'.

The Duke of York's ship

We arrived at the Dock early in the morning, and started to prepare the area for a search of the Dock wall and bottom, to ensure no-one had laid any explosives which may endanger the ships. On this diving operation John was supervisor, I was diver number one, and Jim was my standby diver. Attendants were Brian, Bob, Smoothy and Mick. Also with us was Eileen, a female Police Officer who was on attachment with us prior to applying for the diving unit, and of course our ever willing driver Graham (the Sirocco kid) who was now our permanent driver.

Not only is Graham a good driver, but always mucked in helping us carry the heavy diving gear to the site. I think Graham will fit in well with this close- knit diving unit, he was fit and not afraid of hard work, always had the kettle on for the divers coming out the water and didn't mind our sick sense of humour.

It was decided that I would dive the first area of the dock wall, and Jim dive the second area where HMCS Toronto was to moor. Once dressed in my dry suit, I put my fins on and jumped into the dock. I started to fin along the dock wall, looking up and down for anything unusual. Fortunately I had about 2 feet of visibility, and could see the wall and the bed of the dock at the same time.

After about 40 minutes, and having covered about 300 metres of dock wall, I got a signal on my lifeline to return to the surface. I surfaced and noted I had enough air left to do standby diver for Jim's dive without changing my air bottle. Jim then entered the water and started searching the second area, where the Canadian ship was to moor.

As Jim started his search we could see the Minesweepers entering the lock at the Blackwall entrance. Before Jim had finished his dive, the first minesweeper, HMS

Cottesmore, captained by HRH The Duke of York, had left the lock and was rounding up to come alongside the area we had just searched.

Once we had finished searching, we returned to the lorry for tea and sat and watched the other two minesweepers manoeuvre and moor up. All was well; nothing had gone bang, so we felt we had done our job well.

Shortly after, we saw Prince Andrew come off HMS Cottesmore, dressed in full uniform. As he stepped from the gangway of the ship onto the dock he looked towards our diving lorry. He then walked towards us and stopped, looking in at us drinking tea. There was puzzled look on his face, and then he smiled and made swimming gestures with his arms.

We waved him towards the lorry. 'Are you the divers?' he enquired. 'Yes, police divers; we've just made sure your ship's not in danger,' said Mick.' He then cheekily said, 'Do you want a cup of tea, Guv?'
The Duke of York smiled and replied, 'No thank you, I must go, I'm expecting my mother on board this afternoon.'
And with that jumped into the back of his chauffeur driven Jaguar and sped away.

HRH the Duke of York

Some ten minutes later, the Chief Diving Officer of HMS Cottesmore came along to our lorry and asked what exactly we had searched prior to their arrival, and what it was like in the water. He was quite surprised when we told him we had about 2 feet of visibility. Then the jokes started to fly. Mind the 10 foot pike, and you may find the odd body with a set of concrete boots, and so on. He then told us that he would be putting his divers in every day, one to check their ship and one to have a look at the dock wall and bottom.

We made arrangements to meet him the next day and see if there was any way we could assist with his searches, as we had local knowledge of the dock. That was of course, if we had nothing more serious to deal with.

Friday 20th May, another day another dollar. I arrived at work just before 7am. Nothing had come in during the night before, so we were on for going to West India Dock to assist the Royal Navy divers with their security searches. We arrived at the Dock at 9am, and the Navy divers were already dressed in their diving suits and ready to go. They lowered their inflatable into the dock, the divers got in, and they started their search.

The night before, Mick had been busy on his computer, playing around with the graphics program, and had produced a framed certificate addressed to HRH the Duke of York, from the Met Police Underwater Search Unit, congratulating him on making a reasonable fetch when he brought his ship alongside the Dock.

We asked when Andrew would be back so that we could present it to him, and we were told about 11am. Once the security search was over, we were invited down to the senior rates' mess for a 'wobbly coffee'. A wobbly coffee is a coffee laced with navy rum and very nice it is too. We talked about what we all had in common, diving.

Once all the pleasantries were over, and all our cheeks were glowing with having had numerous wobbly coffees, we were invited to look around the ship and see the diving equipment they use. It took a long time to see all the equipment and as we were looking around the ship we had a phone call from the CID at Cannon Row Police Station, to say they might have a job for us. Apparently they had someone in for murder and believed there might be body bits in a sewer and wanted us to recover them, but they were not sure of the location yet and would phone us back when they had questioned the suspect further.

We carried on looking at the Navy's diving gear, they had Aga breathing equipment that we used ourselves, and then there were re-breather sets that dated back to the year dot. They had surface demand helmets and a one-man decompression chamber that looked like it was built for a midget. They explained a medic or doctor had to slide in horizontally across a stretcher to get to an upright section at the end of the tube where he was supposed to sit with his legs astride the stretcher. The patient would then lie on the stretcher with his head between the legs of the medic.

We all thought this was an awful design and you would have to be very close friends, or very trusting, to squeeze in there together. One comment that came from Brian -

could you imagine if the Medic wants to fart, there's no way the patient can get away from it, lying there between his legs!

We were invited to try it out, but all declined. We thanked our host for showing us round the ship, and the hospitality shown to us, and returned to the Diving Lorry to wait and see if Prince Andrew would turn up so that we could present our certificate to him personally.

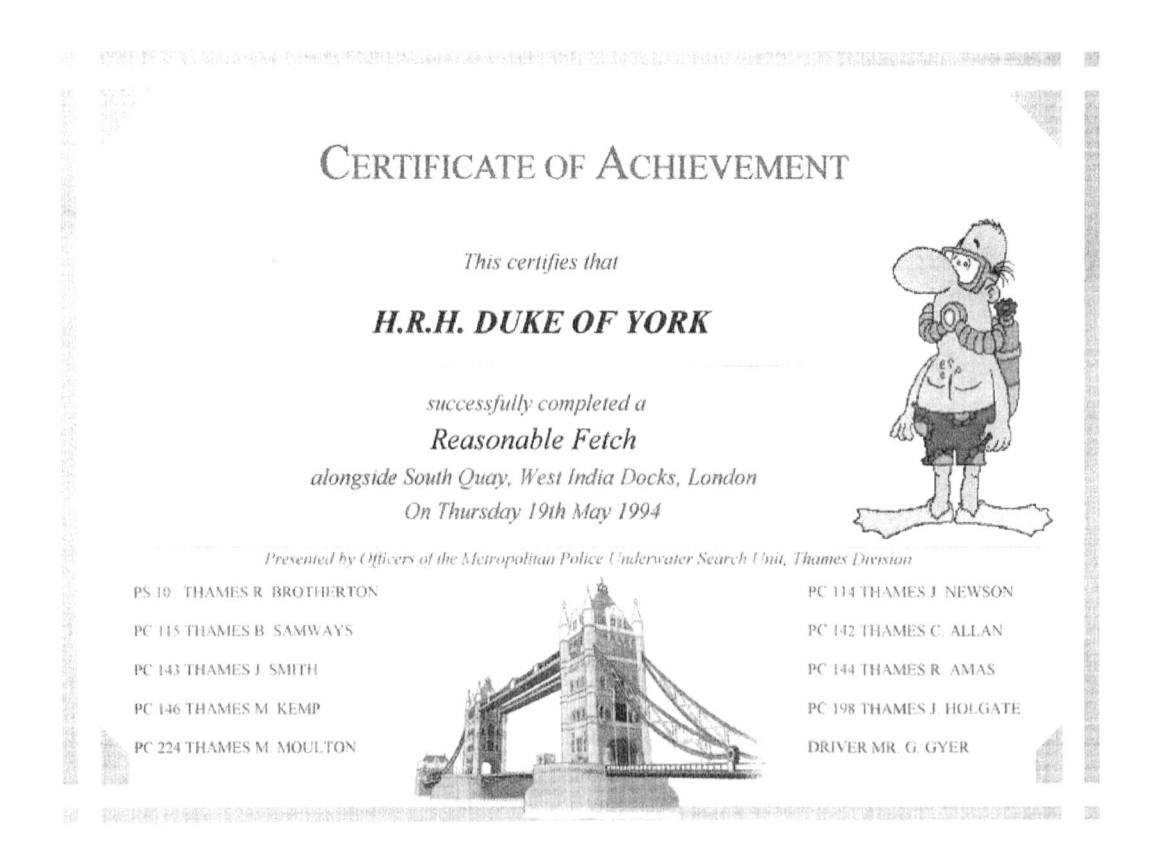

CERTIFICATE OF ACHIEVEMENT

This certifies that

H.R.H. DUKE OF YORK

successfully completed a

Reasonable Fetch

alongside South Quay, West India Docks, London
On Thursday 19th May 1994

Presented by Officers of the Metropolitan Police Underwater Search Unit, Thames Division

PS 10 THAMES R. BROTHERTON	PC 114 THAMES J. NEWSON
PC 115 THAMES B. SAMWAYS	PC 142 THAMES C. ALLAN
PC 143 THAMES J. SMITH	PC 144 THAMES R. AMAS
PC 146 THAMES M. KEMP	PC 198 THAMES J. HOLGATE
PC 224 THAMES M. MOULTON	DRIVER MR. G. GYER

This is the certificate that Mick made for HRH the Duke of York

It was now 12pm. and the Duke of York still had not turned up. We decided we could not wait any longer as we all had jobs to do back at Wapping. Mick and John decided they would go back on board before we left and ask the officers on HMS Cottesmore to present the certificate on our behalf.

Once on board the ship, Mick and John entered the officers Mess where they were having a meal. 'Sorry to bother you,' said Mick, 'but we have got to go and recover some body bits from a sewer, and wondered if you would mind presenting this certificate on our behalf to Prince Andrew?'
Several Officers on hearing this stopped eating; one pushed his meal aside, stood up and said, 'Yes, of course we will. Thank you for your assistance. I don't fancy your next job, it's put me off my meal just hearing about it.'

We returned to Wapping, still waiting for the phone call. After re-filling the air bottles, washing and maintaining the diving gear we adjourned to our Mess for a coffee. It was getting near to 2pm when we were due to go off duty, as we had been on duty since 6am, and were due back on duty at 8pm for more security searches, this time to do with the Centenary Celebrations of the building of Richmond Lock and Weir in 1894. It was being attended by HRH the Duke of York.

At 2pm we all went home. I arrived home feeling tired, knowing I had to go back on duty at 8pm, and thought I would have a sleep for a while. Kay, my wife, had other ideas, and it was not long before we were in bed for the afternoon. It seemed like the blinking of an eye, when I woke and looked at the clock, it showed 6pm. Kay said, 'I had better get you something to eat before you go.'

A nice chilli was soon devoured, and it was time to return to work.

I arrived at work to hear Jim talking on the phone in the office. He was talking to a detective superintendent about the body bits we were asked to search for earlier. It now turned out there was a well in a block of empty Victorian flats, situated opposite New Scotland Yard, and it was believed there might be a body in the well, but access was restricted in that it was at basement level and in an enclosed space. Jim explained we could not do anything this weekend due to the commitments of security searches for Prince Andrew.

By 8pm all the lads had arrived at Wapping. Bob, Jim, John, Mick, Graham our driver and our female contender for the Unit, Eileen. We started to load the lorry with diving gear first, then BA gear in case we had to search any enclosed spaces.

Then the outboard motor had to be lifted onto the lorry. I saw our new outboard lying on the equipment cage floor, and lifted it up to put it onto the trolley. As I lifted it swung awkwardly, and the prop struck the rear of my ankle. I was in agony and said a few choice words, which I thought, might ease the pain.

It was then decided we would take the other outboard that was already on a trolley. I got into the rear of the lorry to take the handles of the trolley as Jim and Graham got either side of it to lift it up to me. Graham is a bit of a weight lifter and a lot stronger than Jim, and as they lifted it up, Graham lifted much faster, causing the outboard to fall over towards Jim and smash against his head. This was not a good start to the evening. Jim staggered, but remained on his feet. 'Are you ok?' asked Graham.
'Of course I'm not bloody alright,' replied Jim, in an angry Scots accent, 'you lifted it too fast.'
There was a nasty bruise and graze to Jim's head, near his eye. 'It bloody hurts, but I'll be ok.'

Once everything we required was loaded up we were on our way to the first search at Tower Pier, just outside the tower of London. The Pier had to be searched first, then the Motor launch `Royal Nore', which was moored at Tower Pier, and was to be used by HRH to convey him to Richmond Lock.

The Royal Nore on the River Thames

When Royalty is on board they are accompanied by the Royal Watermen, shown here in their red uniforms

Brian was the diver for this security search, and Mick his standby. Once on the pier we liaised with security and told them what we intended to do. Brian entered the water and started pulling himself along the edge and underside of the pier until eventually we had searched the whole of Tower Pier, declaring it sterile.

Next was the Royal Nore. Again Brian entered the water and searched around and under the launch. Brian came out of the water, his dry suit covered in green anti-fouling. Graham, our driver was with us during the search, keen to assist as usual, but unfortunately for me as I was crouching down behind him, winding Brian's life line onto the reel, Graham bent down to pick something up, at the same time swinging one of his legs backwards and kicked me straight in the face.

'Oh no,' I thought, as the realization of more pain came over my face, 'I hope this is not going to be the trend for the rest of this operation.'

Graham was most apologetic, but that didn't stop it hurting.

The search on Tower Pier and the Royal Nore done we made our way to Kew Pier, which was further up river, next to Kew gardens. There was the pier and another boat owned by the National Rivers Authority to be searched. When we got to Kew Pier there was no one about to let us onto the Pier, and the gates on the gangway to it were locked. We waited a while, and had time to have a welcome cup of tea.

Once the tea was finished we went to the pier again; still no one about. We could not wait any longer as we had a lot more to do at Richmond Lock. We decided to climb over the wall further up from Kew Pier and lower the gear down for the divers. Mick was the next diver in and he climbed over the wall and slid down the bank onto the foreshore. He then walked to the pier along the foreshore, and on reaching Kew Pier he found the tide was so low that he could walk around the pier to check it. This completed we humped the diving gear back to the lorry and loaded it on board.

Just as we were about to leave the Pier a man turned up, 'I'll just open it up for you,' he said.
 'Too late,' we replied, 'we've already searched it. As far as we are concerned it's ok, and down to you now to keep it sterile. We have to go to Richmond.'

We arrived at Richmond. It was still quite early in the morning and we were all feeling a little bit tired now, but knew there was a lot more work to be done, and the first thing to be done was to unhitch the inflatable dingy trailer from the lorry and launch the inflatable Zodiac. That done, it was time for another coffee and something to eat for those that brought a packed lunch or should I say, breakfast.

The next stage of our Security search would be a long drawn out affair, as there were several pontoons to search and another boat that HRH Prince Andrew would be using when he arrived at Richmond Lock. Mick volunteered to do all the searches at Richmond and John stayed as his standby. Bob supervised and I coxed the Zodiac and worked as one of the diver's attendants together with Jim, when the diving was taking place.

We started by searching a boat called the `Lady Mayors', then a boat called a 'Shallop', which was modelled on the type seen in King Henry the Eighth's day and powered by rowers. Mick rolled over the side of the Zodiac into the water and found he was standing on the bottom looking up at the hull of the shallop, just inches from his head. The water was clear and he could see the whole of the boat's bottom and could also see Jim, his attendant, leaning over the side of the boat.

That completed we went across to the pontoon near Richmond Bridge and started to search there. At the same time Brian and Eileen put on their hard hats and searched the top of the pontoon. That completed, we then had to travel down river to Richmond Lock to search more pontoons. The time was 6am, and the River Thames was already getting busy with river authority craft, Port of London Authority Craft and Thames Police Boats. At the same time, vintage boats of all types were arriving to celebrate the centenary of the opening of Richmond Lock and Weir. The vintage boats were going to form a procession going from Richmond Lock to Richmond Bridge, following the Duke of York who was to be rowed up there after a ceremony at Richmond Lock.

While we were searching the pontoons set up near Richmond Lock, we were called by the lock keeper of Richmond Lock who said, I think there is something on the lock gate sill. It's causing the lock gates to jam open; I think you should check it out. We agreed and hoped it wasn't a suspect object, i.e. a bomb.

We positioned the Zodiac near a ladder that led down onto the sill; this made it easy to follow the line of the sill. After 15 minutes underwater Mick returned to the surface to report that there was a large tyre on the sill, and that he had removed it. The lock gates were checked again and they closed perfectly.

All the required searches were now completed, it was now 8:20am and the river was absolutely boiling with craft of all shapes and sizes, and all with people dressed up in Victorian costumes, a lovely sight to see, but what was sad about this wonderful occasion was the weather. It rained all day long.

We returned to Richmond Bridge where the lorry was parked. Our duty now was to sit and wait until the whole event was over and HRH Andy was safely back on dry land, and whisked away in his car. For the first time for hours we could relax with a cup of tea. It was then we realized how tired we all were.

At about 1:20pm HRH Andy arrived at Richmond Lock on the Royal Nore to make a speech, and to take the salute from the Little Dunkirk Boats. The Royal Nore had not gone bang, so we were pleased we had done our job on that. HRH Andy then carried out all the other duties he had to do, like unveiling a commemorative plaque, lowering the sluices on Richmond Weir and so on.

He was then due to change boats and to be rowed from Richmond Lock in the Shallop boat we had searched earlier, which was moored to the pontoon just below Richmond Bridge. All the rowers were waiting, dressed very smartly in their ancient Waterman uniforms, but soaking wet because of the continuous rain. HRH decided because of the appalling weather he would continue up to Richmond Bridge in the Royal Nore. As he passed our diving lorry, he came out of the cabin of the Royal Nore and waved at us, and made a swimming gesture again, indicating he had not forgotten who we were and what we were doing for his safety. I hope he appreciated the certificate we presented him with on HMS Cottismore.

It then only remained for us to get our Zodiac out of the water, lift it onto the trailer and hitch the trailer to the back of our lorry. This done we started our long journey back to Wapping. Once back at Wapping we unloaded the diving gear, recharged the air bottles, had a welcome shower and headed for home.

I arrived home at 6pm to a tepid welcome. Kay, my wife, was not pleased at being left alone for so long, and thought I should have made an effort to phone her. I do not think she realized how difficult it was to do that on this operation, and security required we not contact anyone during a security operation.

I jumped into a warm bath, and Kay brought me a large glass of whisky. I really felt like going to sleep now, but Kay had prepared a lovely meal of monk fish, wrapped in bacon on a barbeque spike and mixed vegetables.

We sat down to eat and I could not stop talking about the operation. All the mishaps, the injuries and jokes, it all seemed not so serious now. Two bottles of wine later it was 10:00pm and time for bed, I had been awake now for 28 hours.

I woke up the next day and my ankle was so painful, it made walking very difficult, but as the day went on it got a lot better. At least I have Sunday at home with Kay, I thought, and I'll get a good night's sleep tonight. No such luck.

At forty-five minutes past midnight the phone went; it was Fred, the reserve officer at Wapping.
 'Do you want to earn some more money,' he said sarcastically, and as if I had a choice. 'We've got a suspected suicide at Hackney.'
 I sleepily said, 'ok Fred,' and then reached for my watch to see what time it was. It was then I realized there would be no public transport running. I phoned Fred back and said, 'any chance of being picked up by boat Fred?'
'Yes,' he replied, 'Dougy will come down in about 15 minutes.'

'Ok,' I said, 'I'll be on Greenland Pier.' I slowly got dressed, kissed Kay goodbye, and made my way to Greenland Pier.

As I stood waiting I could see the police boat in the distance coming towards me, it then turned into Greenland Dock entrance, I waved my arms, whistled and shouted but obviously Dougy could not hear or see me. As he disappeared into the dock entrance I heard the engine of the police boat stop, and could just see the mast light above the dock wall. He was about 400 yards from where I was standing on Greenland Pier. Now the engine had stopped I shouted again, 'Dougy, over here.'

I whistled and shouted again, much to the annoyance of some of my neighbours who I could now see looking out of their windows.

An all night fisherman was fishing in the entrance to Greenland Dock saw me and cottoned on to the fact I was trying to catch the attention of the police boat.

He ran towards the police boat and I heard him shout, 'he is over there, on the pier.'

I heard the police boat start up, and as it came out of the entrance to Greenland Dock. I stood at the end of Greenland Pier and waved my hand in front of a red navigation light. Dougy saw me and came over.

I jumped on board and said, 'didn't Fred tell you I would be on Greenland Pier?'

'Yes, sorry,' replied Dougy, I thought you were still living on your boat in the marina.'
We raced back to Wapping at 28 knots. I was the first of the diving team to arrive.

I asked the CAD officer to print out the message relating to the possible body, and it showed the location was the

Grand Union Canal, the rear of Orwell Court, Pownal Road E.8. The incident was timed at 9:24pm on 22nd July 1994, and said, believed a female had committed suicide and jumped into the Canal. At 10pm an ambulance was called; 10:18pm Hackney Police were on scene and asked for a dog van to the scene to search the banks of the canal. 10:33pm a Land rover from Traffic department was asked to supply lights to illuminate the scene. At 10:40pm India 99, the police helicopter was asked to attend. Officers on scene were then told yes, it could attend but it will take 1 hour and 30 minutes before they can be airborne. Do you still require it? They said, 'No.'

At 11:06pm Wapping Thames Division were requested. They sent a van with an inflatable dingy to the scene arriving at 11:33pm. Last to be called, as usual, the Underwater Search Unit. I think I have expressed my annoyance in past chapters for the delay in calling the Underwater Search Unit, and looking at the factors involved in the original call, I'm sure most of you reading my story feel the frustration I do. By the time Bob, John, Mick, Chris and Graham arrived at Wapping it was 1:45am.

For this operation, Chris would be number one diver and John number two. We loaded lighting and a generator onto our lorry to illuminate the scene. Arriving at the scene, we were met by two Thames Officers who were called earlier. They explained the story. Apparently the woman who was missing was sitting on the lock gate leverage poles and crying. She was seen by a passer-by who asked her if she was alright; she said, 'fuck off and leave me alone.'

The man said that he turned away and walked off and when he looked back she was not there He feared she had fallen or jumped into the canal.

We surveyed the location and decided because it was so dark the first thing to do was put up our lighting. The lighting pole, which fitted onto a stand, was extended 12 feet into the air. The generator was then started and the lights switched on so now the lock was illuminated.

When diving on locks, the diver must always dive on the low-pressure side. This was well drummed into our brains in diving school with a story about two Scottish police divers that lost their lives diving on the high pressure side of a lock. Those were the days when police diving was in its infancy and there was no Health and Safety regulation or formal Police diver training.

Apparently this is what happened. One of the police officers was called out to a suspected drowning in a lock, and as he was a diver was asked to recover the body. When he arrived at the lock his partner, another police officer who could also dive had not arrived. He decided after waiting some time, to go in alone, and asked someone to hold a line the other end of which he had attached around his waist. When he got to the bottom of the lock he was caught in a current caused by a lock valve not being closed properly, and was sucked against the valve and held there.

He signalled to the surface that he was trapped, but the suction was too great, and he could not be pulled up. Sometime later his colleague arrived and realising there was something wrong, he dived into the lock following his colleague's lifeline down to where he was trapped. He too then suffered the same fate, and both drowned.

We decided we would lay a jackstay 20 yards away from the entrance to the lock gate, and work towards it on the low-pressure side. Chris, now dressed in his diving gear, entered the water and started his search. It was very shallow, only about 4 feet deep and full of rubbish, shopping trolleys, and a pedal cycle.

Eventually Chris reached the lock gate some 20 minutes into his search. We decided to carry on into the lock. We got Chris out of the water, and at the same time Graham, our driver, came over with some nice warm coffee and tea. Well timed Graham. We quickly drank the tea and coffee and started to lay out another jackstay to allow Chris to search the actual lock.

We would still be on the low pressure side as the water in the canal on the other side of the lock gate was the same level as the inside of the lock. We also opened the lock gates as an extra safety precaution. Chris went down the ladder into the lock and started his search again. We were all hoping it would not be long before we had a result. After another 40 minutes, nothing was found.

It was now 3am, we were tired but thought we must give the area a good coverage and so decided to put John in where Chris began his search in front of the lock gate and work away from it. John entered the water and started his search. He was amazed he had a certain amount of visibility, and with the lights shining down on the surface of the water could see the white search line. John searched for an hour but still nothing was found.

Slightly disappointed we decided we could search no more, and that we had covered a large area far in excess of what a body would travel. We packed up our diving equipment and returned to Wapping to grab a couple hours of sleep before we were on duty again. No one knows who the girl was, and no body was ever found, but we can only go on information given, even if it's false, because it may be the truth.

The Well

23rd May 1994

It was 9:15am at Belgravia Police Station, and we were meeting a detective, who told us that he and a team of detectives were investigation the murder of a gay man, who had been strangled. The killer came into the Police Station a few days after the incident and confessed to the murder. Further investigation highlighted the fact that he may be linked to another murder, and it was thought the body might be down a well in derelict buildings that were situated opposite New Scotland Yard.

At 9:30am we left Belgravia Police Station to go to the well. Our team today was Bob, John, Mick, Chris, Brian and me. We arrived at some derelict Victorian buildings called Artillery Mansions, and were told the location of the well, which was in a basement under the buildings, and to get to it we would have to go through a long tunnel, that was dark, damp and dirty.

We decided the two divers who were top of the list would put on overalls, take a couple of lights, and go down to survey the well. The detective led us through the maze of tall Victorian flats. We then found the entrance into the basement went down a winding staircase and proceeded through a maze of dark, damp corridors.

Along one corridor was a narrow gauge railway line and halfway along the railway was a small trolley. We assumed this must have been used as a service tunnel for transporting equipment to the boiler room. After about 200 yards of corridor we came to a doorway to our right, and saw an immense boiler room, and there was asbestos everywhere. We could also see light coming into the boiler room from a window that was situated at ground level. This would make good access if we were able to remove grating covering the window.

The corridor continued on from the entrance to the boiler room for about another 30 feet, and this section was piled high with rubbish, consisting of rotten wood, paper, rusty metal and old asbestos that had fallen off heating pipes.

Brian and I cleared some of the rubbish, and saw the well at the end of the corridor. We looked down the well with our torches shining through the clear water; at the same time water was dripping from the ceiling on our heads and down our necks. The well was cluttered with iron pipes and wood, but we could see part of the bottom through this mess.

Our next job was to plumb the depth of the well, and do a survey. From the edge of the well it was 6 feet to the water, and then the water then went 12 feet to the bottom of the well. Access was going to be extremely difficult. We were going to need lots of lighting and all the debris would have to be removed before a diver could be put down the well. In its present state it was far too dangerous.

We got in touch with the Met Police special operations department and found out they had a mini underwater video camera that would be ideal for surveying the well before risking the life of a diver. The other major hazard we were concerned about was the asbestos that seemed to be lying all over the place.

As we had all been on duty since one in the morning, we were now all very tired, and it would be stupid to start the operation today. Before returning to our base at Wapping, and as we were so near Tintagel House (the headquarters of the Force Health and Safety Executive Officer), we decided to give him a call to ask about the hazards involved.

Geoff Lloyd was the senior HSE man, and on consulting Geoff he suggested we should use filter masks, Hard Hats, and protective goggles. I wish he had told Brian and me before we went in to survey the well! Geoff Lloyd had some filter masks that he let us have there and then. We had the rest of the equipment required back at Wapping.

We returned to Wapping feeling pretty knackered, and hoped we would be off on time today. About 2:45pm, 15 minutes before we were due to go off duty, the phone rang. All our hearts stopped momentarily. Oh no, not another job. A gun had been thrown in a canal.

Bob used his common sense, and put it off, saying, 'The lads have been on duty since 1 am and we are all very tired. We have a possible murder job tomorrow so we will do your job on Wednesday.'

We all breathed a sigh of relief and then raced for the door before the phone went again.

The Well Continued

24th May 1994

I arrived at Wapping at 6am today. We were due to explore the well that we surveyed the previous day.

The team today consisted of Bob, Jim, John, Mick, Brian, Chris and me. After a quick breakfast, we loaded the lorry with as many lights as we could muster, plus a small petrol generator and the new B.A (Breathing Apparatus) gear we had recently acquired for using in enclosed spaces.

On arrival at the scene we were met by the CID, and a camera crew from Thames Television who were following the operations of the murder squad. Also at the scene were the Met Police senior safety officer, Geoff Lloyd, and the special operations team with the mini underwater video camera we intended to use.

We all got dressed in blue overalls and yellow hard hats and started to unload the diving gear, light, and generator from our lorry to take to a location close to the well entrance. The first task was to clear the passageway to the well.

Jim and I were top of the diving list, so were first to go in and clear the passageway. A plan was formulated to work in teams of four to clear the wood and asbestos. Those closest to the well would wear protective goggles, and filter masks to prevent breathing in the dust and asbestos particles. We would also have to take our gas monitor to check the air quality.

Bob, Jim and I went into the basement via a steel door we had managed to break open. This led into the large boiler room, which then led to the tunnel that got us to the well head. The first thing we started to do was set up the lighting.

It was dark, dirty and very dusty in the boiler room, and there was blown asbestos from the pipes and boilers everywhere. Once the lights were set up, we started the generator and hey presto we had light.

We walked slowly down the damp corridor, looking all the time at the floor, and trying to avoid stepping on sharp pieces of metal and wood. Eventually we got to the wellhead. We started shifting the rubbish that consisted of asbestos sheets, wood of all shapes and sizes, rusty metal and barbed wire.

As Bob, Jim and I were in the tunnel passing out the debris to John who was at the end of the tunnel near the boiler room, there was suddenly a loud beep, beep, beep, and we saw the red light was flashing on the Gas detector. We looked at each other in horror. Bob who was carrying the detector reacted immediately, and shouted through his gas mask, 'out, Out, OUT.'

We all turned and ran as fast as was possible through and over the rubbish in the tunnel, into the boiler room, and through and back up to the ground level. When we got our breath back we looked at the Gas detector, the oxygen level had dropped from 21.3% to 17.3%, and had we stayed there and let it drop to 17% we would all have been unconscious and possibly close to death.

It was decided we would have to use BA equipment. We could link this with our surface demand reel, and that would give us an endless supply of air while we were working.

Jim and I dressed in the BA equipment and linked up to the surface demand reel via an inlet on the 1st stage of the BA gear. We were then linked by a buddy air umbilical. We also had to have communications and that had to be connected and trailed along with the airline.

Our first job, now we had the BA equipment on, was to go back to the wellhead and check out for air quality, and explosives. Jim and I started down the stairs into the basement. The generators started up and we had light.

Progress through the boiler room was slow as we had to feed the air and communication line behind us, and not forget we were also linked by a buddy airline. The line kept getting snagged as we negotiated machinery and corners, so Bob and Brian put on Aga diving sets and came into the boiler room to feed the lines behind us.

Eventually we reached the well-head. Headroom was about 5 feet and the ceiling was dripping like rain. I switched the Gas monitor to explosives, and it registered 0%, that was a relief. I then switched to Air quality.

I could see it start to decrease immediately, 21.3% to 20.7%, then the alarm started to sound and the red light flashed, reflecting in Jim's mask. He didn't look very happy. The oxygen level went down to between 18.5% and 17.3% and kept hovering at these levels. I reported back to the surface telling them what our findings were.

Mick who was supervising this operation asked us to return to the boiler room to collect the TV camera that we were going to put down the well. The camera consisted of a very small tubular body about 8 inches long and about 2 inches in diameter, with a lens on the end. This was fitted into an aluminium `U' frame, and just above that was a powerful light. This then screwed into a long pole to keep the camera rigid. The pole could then be screwed into other poles to extend the length.

Jim took control of the camera so that I was free to communicate with the surface. On the surface the camera was linked to a television screen and video recorder.

We again made our way back to the well head, trailing all the wire and air hose behind us. Just as we got there, off went the Gas alarm again. We were getting used to it now, and it didn't make us jump so much. At the same time as this happened, Mick called me on the radio and said, 'you have already breathed down 240 bar of air; we are going to change over to the next bottle. Let me know if you feel anything.'
'Ok' I replied, 'will standby.'
'Ok' said Mick, 'did you feel the change over?'
'No' I replied.
'Ok.' said Mick, 'lower the camera into the well slowly.'

I shouted at Jim through my mask to lower the camera slowly into the well. As he started to do this, Mick called again. 'Let us know when it's in the water Mac, and we can put the light on.'
The reason for this was, if the light was put on before it was in the water, it may burn out, not having the water to cool it.
'OK.' I replied, 'we are just putting the second extension on. It's now in the water.'

The light came on and illuminated the well showing bright colours of rust, yellow and green slime and shimmering clear water.

'Perfect,' said Mick, 'we have a good picture of it going down the well.' He then continued, 'Have you reached the bottom yet?'

'No.' I replied, 'we need another extension.'

There wasn't one, so we were asked to turn the camera downwards.

The special operations team working on the monitor and video on the surface intervened, and said this was not possible unless we had the right spanner and a pair of pliers. We didn't, so Mick called back, 'Return to the surface so that they can adjust the camera.'

By now Jim and I had been working on air for over an hour, and Mick asked if we would like to change over and have a blow on the surface. Everyone agreed this was a good idea, so we adjourned to the USU lorry for a quick 10 minutes tea break. John invited the ITV camera crew in for tea with us, and at the same time produced some small badges of police divers that he was selling for charity.

John has a knack of making people feel guilty if they don't buy one, but it's all for a good cause, Handicapped Children. He has been selling them for some time now and has raised a lot of money, although I thought the latest design of badge showing a police diver coming out of a toilet was more towards the police sense of humour, but it is also very significant with some of the places we have to dive in I suppose.

Tea finished and a lot of laughing and joking about the alarm going off, we returned to the job in hand. This time, Bob and Brian put on the BA gear linked to the surface demand airline, and Chris and John dressed in Aga diving gear to feed their airline through the boiler room and corridor.

As well as repositioning the angle of the camera, we also decided to tape an extra length of wood onto the poles to give extra reach.

The second team slowly made their way back to the well head. Once there the camera was slowly lowered to the bottom. We could now see the well on the monitor from a different angle, and managed to cover the whole of the well. It also showed there was a pipe leading into the well that was probably the water feed, but too small for a body to slip past.

When the surface team was satisfied that the whole of the well was covered and there definitely was no body down there, the camera was pulled back up to the surface.

We could now see Bob and Brian, as the camera was pointing at their faces. Mick told them on the radio, 'we can see you both.'
 Suddenly they burst into song, waving their hands to and fro in unison, singing, 'Always look on the bright side of life, Bdom, Bdom, Bdom.'

We were in fits of laughter on the surface. 'Are you lot always like this?' asked one of the TV camera crew. 'Yes,' I replied with a smile, 'with the sort of jobs we have to do you can't be too serious or you would end up having a nervous breakdown.'

'Ok, that's enough,' said Mick, 'return to the surface.'

During the hour Bob and Brian were down there we changed three bottles of air on the surface demand in one hour. I think we were all pleased in a way, that there was not a body down the well, mainly because of the enclosed space at the well head, and the amount of machinery and rubbish that would have to be negotiated by the diver before he would be able to reach the bottom.

The adrenalin was flowing; we had all enjoyed the experience of doing something different and challenging, with a little element of danger. The CID were happy, and the special events team were pleased they had a chance to use their expensive TV camera and video monitor.

Enclosed space searching was now as much a part of our duties as diving, but I was pleased that in a few years time I would be retiring from the police force and would not have to do them anymore. I joined the unit to dive and saw the enclosed space searching as a money saving exercise by the police authorities, using us for both roles, rather than setting up another specialized unit.

Enclosed spaces training day

7ᵀᴴ June 1994

Today we were due to meet the training officers for Thames Water at Hammersmith, as part of our ongoing training for working in enclosed spaces. The Thames water officers said they were going to put us in one of their worst sewers to test our claustrophobia and if we got through that without incident, give us a tour of the normal six-foot sewer in that area.

At 8:30am we arrived at Thames water headquarters in Hammersmith, and were met by two training officers. We first we went into their office where we were briefed on what we were going to do today, and the safety procedures we would all have to abide by. They supplied the equipment we would all use, which consisted of overalls, hard safety hat, waders with lead studded soles (lead so that no sparks could be caused, as lot of sewers contain explosive gas), a harness, a miner's lamp, and lastly the most important piece of equipment, the bail-out set, nicknamed the Turtle, because the shape of the stainless steel cover on it looked exactly the same shape as a turtle shell.

The bail-out set was demonstrated to us by one of the Thames Water officers. A clip that held the turtle shaped casing together was first pushed. This caused the cover to fall off onto the ground. You were then left with an air bag, fitted to a filter. On the other side of the filter was an air hose about eighteen inches long with a mouthpiece on the end, also attached to the mouthpiece was a nose clip. To start using it to breathe, you first removed a plug that was pushed into the mouthpiece. The plug was there to stop sewerage getting into the mouthpiece if you dropped it.

You had to take three deep breaths, on each breath filling the plastic bag previously mentioned. The three breaths now in the filled plastic bag were re-breathed through the filter, taking out harmful gases, and allowed you to breathe for a further half to one hour, this dependent on how heavy your breathing was. Hopefully this would give you enough time to get out of the sewer. The only drawback with this type of breathing apparatus was, if you drew too hard on the breathing tube the apparatus got hot.

As we continued our briefing the one and only mobile phone we had rang. (The rest of us had pagers for an emergency call out). It was Smoothy on the phone who said, in a flustered voice, 'Where are you, I've been going round and round Hammersmith roundabout, and can't find the place.' I started to give Smoothy directions, but was rudely interrupted by Dick (nicknamed 'Excuse Me') who was giving me instructions to give to Smoothy over my instructions to Smoothy. I gave up trying to cope with this two-way conversation and handed the phone to Dick, saying, 'Excuse me, if you know better then get on with it.'

When the briefing was over, we were taken to the equipment room where everyone was issued with the necessary safety equipment. Now all dressed, we were ready to go and carry out the first exercise, which was to climb down a thirty foot ladder into a 100 metre long sewer. It was intended that a qualified sewer worker would lead us through the sewer in groups of five.

Just as we were about to leave, Smoothy turned up. We had given up all hope of seeing him by now, and expected to receive a message saying he had committed suicide on Hammersmith roundabout. 'Wait for me,' he shouted. 'I want to come with you and take some video of our training down the sewer.'
 We all made appropriate noises, and rude remarks about him being late, but waited while he was kitted out. Just before we left, Smoothy had to sign a dispensation form, allowing him to take his video camera down the sewer.

On arrival at the sewer entrance we were all asked again whether we had anything that may cause a spark, for example, a lighter or anything electrical. As Smoothy wanted to video the exercise it was suggested he go the other end of the three foot six inch high sewer, and film it as we emerged the other end, it being too narrow and dirty to go in with a video camera.

John, Dick, Jim, myself and Richard Delapole, who was a Thames officer on attachment to the diving unit for a week, prior to appearing on the selection board for a new members of the unit, were the first to go. We started to go down the ladder into the narrow sewer. 'Only one man at a time on the ladder,' shouted a Thames Water sewer man, and continued, 'just in case anyone falls on the safety man at the bottom.'

Just before it was my turn to go down the ladder, one of the Thames Water instructors said to me,
 'Of course we don't usually go down these sewers now, because the union say for safety reasons we are not allowed to go in a sewer under four feet high.' !

As we started to crawl through the sewer on our hands and knees, we stirred up the three or four inches of brown liquid in the sewer, and you could smell the methane gas, it was awful. I found it difficult to breathe and thought the gas alarm is going to go off any minute.
It didn't and we continued on towards the exit a hundred metres on.

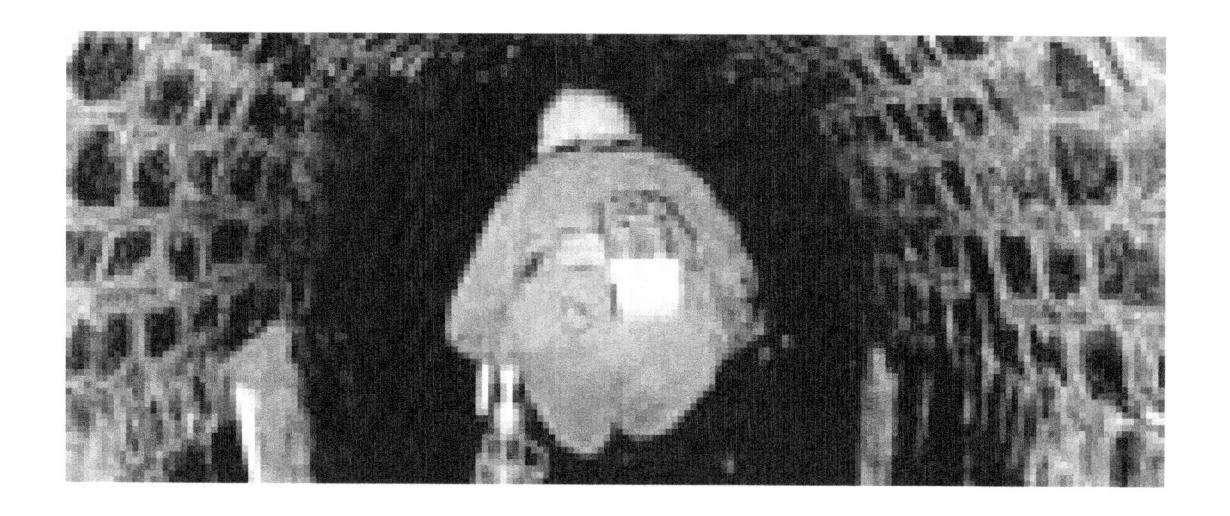

It got hotter, I felt something brush past my hand, then my face caught a spider's web and I could see all the roof of the narrow sewer was covered in webs with large spiders inside. I started to sweat and felt claustrophobic, and it felt as if the sewer was never going to end.

I wondered if I was the only one feeling this way, or whether the others felt the same.

As we emerged out of the sewer into a chamber where you could stand up, I looked at the others emerging from the narrow section. Dick's eyes seemed to be popping out his head, and he was sweating profusely.
'Did you enjoy that Dick?' I asked.
He replied with, 'No I bloody didn't, crawling through shit is not my idea of fun.'

Once everyone was safely out the sewer and into the chamber, we climbed back to the surface, one at a time.

This part of our exercise over, we stood in the road near the manhole, covered in brown muck, brushing the spiders and what appeared to be large wood lice off our overalls. We were told the next part of our exercise would be a lot easier, as the sewer was six feet in diameter, but we had to climb down a ladder 60 feet long to get to it, and I hate heights.

Eventually all were assembled at the bottom of the ladder. It was very dark, apart from what we could see in the beam of the lights attached to our helmets. The smell was bad but bearable as we started to walk along the sewer, led by a Thames Water sewer man, not knowing where we were going or what we may encounter.
Someone started singing, 'Always look on the bright side of life, bdum, bdum, budm,' then everyone else joined in.
The sewer man leading us looked back. I think he thought we were a little bit eccentric!
The sewage was about a foot deep, and one of us asked,
'How deep does it get?'
The Thames Water man shone his hand held torch to the ceiling of the sewer and pointed. Stuck to the brickwork were condoms, tampons, toilet paper and other rubbish. He explained that when it rains anywhere in London, you have to get out quick.

'The first thing you feel is a rush of air, just like when a tube train comes into a station. If you ignored it and stayed in the sewer, the next thing you would see is a wall of water coming towards you.'

We continued along the dark smelly sewer, passing junctions now and then, going off to the right and left of the sewer we were in. We all hoped the sewer man knew where we were in the sewer, because we didn't have a clue. Unknown to us he had missed a turning. Smoothy must have sensed this and said to him, 'Should we have turned right back there?'
The Thames Water man stopped and thought for a few seconds, and said, 'Yes I think we should have, thank you.'

It was then about turn and back the other way. Eventually we came to the junction we should have turned at, that led into a large chamber, that was as large as the dome of St Paul's Cathedral. The Thames Water man explained that this chamber they call a sump, could fill up in five minutes, and then pumps would start up and pump the excess water somewhere else

After what seemed like an hour, we arrived at a manhole where we were going to exit the sewer. To our surprise it was right outside Thames Water headquarters. We then changed and showered and were treated to lunch provided by Thames Water.

At lunch we were asked what we thought of the exercise and if there were any questions we wanted to ask. I asked about rescue procedures. I was surprised to learn that unless the person was in immediate danger, they called out the fire brigade. But now, once we were fully trained they would call us.

The day ended with Thames water presenting us with a statue of Old Father Thames. We thanked them for a very enlightening day and retuned to the diving unit head quarters at Wapping Police Station.

Training for security searching

We had been doing security searches for some time in the USU but now we had taken on the added responsibility of doing enclosed space searches, which could include anything from a sewer, to a drain or anywhere where breathing apparatus may be needed.

Our first training was with Thames Water Authority who taught us to use a bail out set. This consisted of a set that was similar to a re-breather where the air you breathe out is cleaned and you breathe it in again and again. The re-breather would only be put on if the gas/chemical alarm each man carried went off, indicating there was some sort of gas that may cause asphyxiation.

Once we were trained to use this equipment we carried out a practice operation in underground sewers and passages in Reading. This was a joint operation with other Underwater Search Units.

The army bomb disposal team had set up small explosive charges in the sewer that fortunately would make more noise than anything else if triggered. There were different types of triggering devices on each explosive, and all were hidden. They could range from trip wires to light sensors so we had to be extremely careful where we trod, and shone our torches.

Each Underwater Search Unit had to complete a plan the night before, and we sat up most of the night planning in-between the odd drink or three. When we turned up at the entrance to the sewer we had a yellow cut out canary tied to the end of a stick. The army and police personnel monitoring our performance asked why we had a paper canary dangling from the stick? We all laughed and said it was our gas detector! This was not taken very well by the senior police officers, and we were told this was a serious matter and not to joke about this sort of thing.

But the army bomb disposal officers did have a smile on their face.

We knew how serious it was, it was our lives on the line when we were searching for real explosives but if we didn't have a bit of humour in our job we would not be able to cope and probably end up spending more time with a psychiatrist than doing the job.

Not being put off we lowered the gas detector into the sewer entrance and it showed it was clear. Then we lowered the cut our canary into the entrance hole. We could see the police senior officers were livid, one going very red, but the army bomb disposal officers were covering their mouth with their hands trying hard not to burst out laughing.

We found all ten explosives in the half mile of sewer and surprised the Police and Army bomb disposal team marshals. It was 1992, the biggest threat at this time was the IRA, but there were many other factions that were prepared to blow people up for their cause, and they were using more and more sophisticated explosives. We were told even we were on the list to be blown up as we were classed as part of the anti terrorist department.

When we left our headquarters in Wapping each day, we would first look for any unusual vehicles parked in the road outside the police station. We always looked under our diving lorry to see if there was anything unusual attached to the underside or wheel arches, and when we left we never took the same route to a location.

Things were getting serious and we needed more training in explosives and identification. We were not trained to defuse the explosives, just look for them. That was the job of the Royal Navy Bomb Disposal Team, who we had worked and socialized with on many occasions.

A date was set for us to attend a location in Kent close to the Medway River. We were given directions in a sealed envelope and our team set off in the diving lorry towards Kent. We got to what we thought was the location but could not find it. There was a phone number with the instructions and we phoned to tell them where we were, and asked where we should go.

We were told to just stay where we were and someone would find us and lead us to the location.

After the lecture we were shown their museum, which was a real eye opener as to what was currently being used, and they said contrary to general opinion the USSR had more up to date and accurate weapons than the west. I would love to tell you more but I am and always will be bound by the official secrets act.

After a lovely lunch we were taken to a small lake that was about ten meters deep and very muddy with nil visibility. We were split into teams and told to dive down a shot line and just with feel with our hands around the explosive, come up and explain or draw what we had felt. The one with the spikes on was very easy, but others were more difficult; some with fins, some without, some were long and some dumpy like a barrel.
It was a good experience and learning process and we went back to our headquarters at Wapping all the wiser.

We all knew we were volunteers and knew the risk involved each time we carried out an underwater or enclosed space security search, and we were paid exactly the same as an ordinary police officer. But this did not stop us wanting to do our job as a police diver. I think all of us enjoyed the excitement of the unknown and the close knit unit that was unique in the police force. We all had to trust and rely on each other to stay alive.

Remand Prisoner Drowns

2oth July 1994

I woke today with a thick head, and looked out of the window at the river, which was shimmering in the morning sun, it was 6am and it was already hot and sticky. I knew we were going to the grand Union Canal, near Wedlake Street, where we had been diving, looking for a Samurai Sword used in a murder.

I arrived at Wapping Police Station at 7am, and most of the lads were already there having toast and tea. Graham, Bob and I decided we would have 40 minutes training in the Gym, it seemed like a good idea at the time but it was so hot it was an effort to exercise.

At 8:20am the phone rang in our office and Bob, still sweating from the exercising, ran to answer it. He returned to the mess where we all waited to hear whether our plan for today had changed. Bob smiled, the sweat still dripping from his face, 'It's all change lads, and we have a body to look for at Banbury Reservoir.'

As it was a reservoir we had to search, and the location would be a bit vague, we decided to hitch up the inflatable Zodiac's boat trailer. With that done, we climbed aboard and headed for Banbury Reservoir.

We checked the diving list and found that Chris was the last to dive so he would be supervisor for this operation. That was how the system worked now, so that everyone who was qualified as a dive supervisor would get a chance to supervise a dive, no matter what his or her seniority in the diving unit.

On arrival at Banbury Reservoir we were first met by the man in charge of the water sports centre which is on Banbury Reservoir, then the Detective Chief Inspector who was in charge of the case. The Chief Inspector explained that they had found a pile of clothing by the side of the reservoir, and on the clothing was correspondence relating to someone who had been arrested recently by police, and then bailed to attend court at a later date. His relatives said they had not seen him since he was arrested by police, and so the Chief Inspector could see all sorts of allegations being made against Police.

He pointed to his left, to a spot some 800 yards from where we were standing, and said that's where we should start the search, as that's where the clothing was found. We said, 'ok, we will move our diving lorry around there, and start to set up the dive.'

We were just about to leave when the person in charge of the Water Sports centre said, 'The clothing was found over there near the life buoy,' pointing in a completely different direction to where the Chief Inspector indicated.

We turned and looked at the Chief Inspector, whose face went red with embarrassment. We laughed, he laughed, and said, 'ah well, I was never very good at navigation.'

It now having been established that this was indeed the correct location to start our search, we located ourselves where the clothing was found.

Chris came up with the idea of using a four-man 'necklace' around the edge of the reservoir, starting just before the point where the clothing was found. We all agreed that, because there was reasonable visibility in the reservoir, it would be a good idea. Although the diving supervisor has the final say in any diving operation, most decisions made in our unit are by committee.

The four divers at the top of the list started to change; they were Jim, Brian, Mick and Bob. It was really hot now, well up in the 80's. I stripped my shirt off and started to carry the diving equipment up a very steep grassy bank to the reservoir, when suddenly India 99, the police helicopter appeared, coming in low over the reservoir. We had been told that the helicopter might be over at some time today to assist in the search using an infra Red Camera.

The helicopter circled several times over the wrong area, I tried to raise them on the Radio to redirect it nearer the location we were going to dive, but there was no reply. MP (the call sign for New Scotland yard Information Room Control) would say MP to USU or whatever the call sign was, but could not raise them. I could see the Detective Chief Inspector at the dive location on top of the bank, waving his hands furiously at the helicopter, trying to direct them to search where he was.

Graham and Chris and I carried on taking the diving equipment up the steep bank to the dive location. We then saw the helicopter start to descend and land close to our dive location. The helicopter police observer, dressed in black overalls, got out and climbed up the bank towards the Chief Inspector, I could see they were talking, and pointing to the reservoir. Then the Chief Inspector started to shout, 'the body, the body, we can see it under the water over here.'
 I relayed the message by shouting back to the divers, who were still changing.

All the divers jumped out of the lorry in various states of undress and started to run up the bank to the dive location. Bob was still in his underpants as he ran towards the Chief Inspector and the helicopter observer.

Once there we could just see the back of a naked man about 30 yards out from the bank and possibly 4 to 5 feet under the water.

Bob then turned to speak to the helicopter observer, and suddenly realised it was a women police officer. Bob went red, and looked suitably embarrassed, saying, 'Sorry, I didn't realise,' and placed his hands in front of his crutch.

She looked him up and down, smiled and said, 'that's ok, I understand.'

There was now no need for us to do a necklace search, and it would be down to the diver who was top of the list to recover the body, and that was Jim. He got his diving equipment on and started to wade into the water towards the body, then disappeared under the water. It took only 5 minutes for him to locate the body, check it out for murder weapons possibly sticking out or near the body, then to pull it into the shore.

We laid the body, which appeared to be an old man possibly around 60 years of age, onto a white body sheet. He still had rigor mortis, and was in what we called the water skiing position, knees slightly bent and hands straight out at ninety degrees to his torso. Although he was only in for possibly 2 to 3 days, he smelt rather ripe.

We joked about how to get the body over to the other side of the reservoir where the ambulance would turn up.

It was suggested by one of our divers that as there was a water sports centre here and as the body was in the water skiing position, we strap a couple of skis on his feet and tow him across. Another suggested if we stuck a sail in the appropriate place we could sail him across.

It probably sounds very disrespectful to joke like this about someone that has just drowned, but when you have to deal with so many tragic deaths in our line of work, the physiological effect can be quite traumatic if you do

not take a light hearted view of each incident. However as I have mentioned before this is very hard to do when children are involved, and has affected all of us at some time in our diving career.

The Detective Chief Inspector phoned his police station to arrange for the local police surgeon to attend the scene. The conversation went like this. 'What, one hour, that's ridiculous, he will be rotting away in this heat in one hour, he smells bad enough now, tell the doctor it's urgent.'

Five minutes later the Chief Inspector's mobile phone rang again. The doctor could not come out to certify death until he had finished surgery.

The Chief Inspector went mad and said, 'There are 400 children sailing and water skiing on this reservoir so do something quick.'

He turned back to us and said, 'Well it looks like just a straight suicide doesn't it?'

Brian replied, 'What about this blood, coming from the back of his head then?'

Bob said, 'and this knife in his back?'

The wind up continued with others joining in. 'What, where?' said a panic stricken looking Chief Inspector. Then he realised we were joking again, and said, 'You've done your job and thanks very much, now why don't you fu…', then realising the woman police helicopter observer was still with us, he continued with, 'go away.'

As we left, we saw the Chief Inspector and two police officers who had turned up. The Chief Inspector said, 'You and the helicopter observer must have the best job in the Met, I'm stuck here with this stinking stiff, and you swan off for a cup of tea.'

The observer climbed back into the helicopter, politely declining request from the divers for rides, and took off, blowing grass bits everywhere, which was not very good for the eyes and those with hay fever.

Once we re-hitched the trailer with the inflatable dinghies back onto the lorry, we made our way back to the sailing centre and spoke to the man in charge. He asked if we had any time to spare to look for sailing equipment that had been lost overboard in the past. We had an hour to spare, and thought it would be good police public relations to help out and recover their gear.

We dived for an hour and recovered rudders, sailing booms and a launching trolley, this was put down as valuable lost property recovered and returned to the owner. The water sports centre manager was well pleased and said if we ever fancied a stress break we were always welcome to come back and have a go at water skiing, or sailing.

We all returned to Wapping feeling a little tired, hot and sweating profusely in the heat of the day. Although late back we didn't claim for overtime, we call it swings and roundabouts, some you win some you lose.

Dog Bite

29th July 1994

It was Friday 29th July, the last day of the week, and I was looking forward to a peasant weekend off. We had a nice job today looking for a stolen water pump that was believed to have been thrown in the River Thames at Shepperton.

We arrived at Desbrough Island and were met by a Thames Division police boat. After all of the diving equipment was loaded on board the police boat we were ferried across to a barge owned by Thames Water Authority. They had been dredging a tributary off the river Thames, called Desborough Cut.

John was number one diver today and Smoothy his standby. Dick was supervising and Mick, Chris, Bob and I were attendants. John dived for an hour around the crane barge that was moored in the centre of the channel but could not find any trace of the pump. It was decided that we search around and under another barge moored just opposite the crane barge, and against the West bank of Desborough cut.

While the others set up the search pattern for Smoothy to dive, I went onto the embankment to check the mooring lines were secure, before he entered the water. Whilst I was checking the lines I heard the sound of dogs barking.

I looked up and saw two large dogs, that looked like greyhounds running towards me, one was light brown and the other dark brown. Their leads were trailing behind them, and the owner not in sight. They sounded quite ferocious and I thought if I ran they would sense my fear and attack me. I froze and stood perfectly still so as not to excite or frighten the dogs, and remembered someone saying do not look into their eyes or they will see that as a threat. As the dogs got to me I shouted 'stay' in a commanding voice.

The dark brown dog stopped and stood there barking at me but the light brown dog did not, and bit me on my right thigh, puncturing my trousers and skin. I immediately felt extreme pain, and pushed the dog's head away, and tried to keep calm, shouting again, 'Stay.' Both dogs remained about two feet away, at times trying to get near me. Each time they tried, barking and gnashing their teeth, I shouted 'STAY' in a loud voice.

I was hoping my colleagues on the barge would hear the noise, they were not that far away, but they seemed oblivious to what was going on. It was probably only minutes but seemed like ages before the owner appeared around the corner. The dogs were still barking and growling and baring their teeth. I shouted to the owner of the dogs, who was now about some 200 yards away, 'Call your dogs off.'

He did not seem to realise the urgency of my shouts, and just walked calmly towards me and said in a camp voice, 'What seems to be the matter?' I was angry at his calmness and total unconcern that my trousers were ripped and my leg bleeding profusely. I tried to keep calm and not lose my temper with him and said, 'Your dog has bitten me on the leg; can't you see it's bleeding?'
He calmly replied in an unconcerned voice, 'Oh dear, you must have frightened them, they would not hurt anyone.'

As he held his dogs back from me, now on their leads I said, 'Look I'm in extreme pain and I will have to report this, I'm a police officer on duty.'
Now in a very concerned voice he replied, 'Oh no, no, please. It must be the heat, they would not hurt anybody. Please don't report it, you know what their like these days, they will put the dogs down if you report it.'

After getting the owner of the dogs to tie their leads to a tree, preventing them from running off again, I led the owner onto the barge where the rest of the diving team were, and explained what had happened. I pulled my trousers down to reveal a bite with about five puncture wounds, all bleeding and bruising around the bite. The owner of the dogs, in a very camp voice said,

'Oh look dear, I've got some pink cream at home. Let me go back and get it, and I'll put it on the bite but please don't report this, please.'

Still trying to keep calm, I replied, 'I'm sorry but it has to be reported as I have been injured on duty and the bite may cause complications later.'

After reporting the owner, he left with his dogs.

It caused some amusement amongst the team and they tried to cheer me up with some old doggy jokes. On returning to the diving lorry, Dick got out the first aid kit and cleaned the wound with surgical spirit, then dressed it with a dry bandage. I then used our mobile phone to contact my doctor who checked my records and said I was up to date with my tetanus injection and did not need to have another one. The doctor suggested I keep an eye on the bite, and if it got really bad to go and see him.

I then had to go to Sunbury Police Station where I reported the dog bite to a police constable, who also asked to see the wound. I dropped my trousers just as a woman police officer was coming into the office. I blushed, she smiled, and said, 'Don't worry I have seen worse legs than that in here.'

We returned to Wapping Police Station where I then had to fill in an injury on duty report. I was on leave the following two days so did not bother to report sick but on the Monday the bite was still sore and swollen, and my foot started to swell up. I was off sick for two weeks before the swelling and pain disappeared.

I still have hard scar tissue where the dog, which I now know was a Saluki, bit me, and next time the mooring lines have to be checked I will send someone else to do the job, once bitten twice shy.

Some months later I was at court giving evidence against the dog owner. It was revealed that the dogs had bitten someone before me and therefore were liable to be put down. The magistrate presiding over the case asked me if I thought he should order the dogs to be put down. My wound had healed now and to me it's the owner not the dogs that are usually the cause of this type of problem.

I asked the magistrate if the dogs could be spared, but an order made for them to wear muzzles and to be always on a lead when outside the owner's home. This was done, and the magistrate commended my leniency.

Christabel Boyce

1985

It was early in 1985, my pager went off and I was asked to attend Wapping Police Station. On arrival I went into the station office and was told we had a job to search the River Lee. Seven members turned out for the search and we got into the diving lorry and made our way to the location, where we were met by the local CID. They said we were to look for plastic shopping bags that may contain body parts.

This part of the river Lea was very shallow and reasonably clear so we formed a line across the river and started a sweep search. We searched for several hours, recovering hands, and pieces of flesh.

The C.I.D related to us the story.

Nicholas Boyce, after a while decided to confess to his crime, and went into his local police station telling them he had killed his wife and cut her up. The officer on the front desk thought he was some kind of nutter and told him to go away. Nicholas Boyce returned with a solicitor, so now the police had to take him seriously.

He gave a statement with very precise detail and locations where he had disposed of Christabel. Apparently Nicholas Boyce, the husband of Christabel Boyce, (who was a former Nanny to Lord Lucan, who it was alleged murdered the Nanny after Christabel) had killed his wife in a fit of anger, saying he just snapped, punched her and she fell and hit her head and died. He panicked, dragged her body to the bathroom and proceeded to cut up her body to dispose of her. All this was done while his two children were in the flat.

The hands, breasts and other bits of flesh were found in the River Lee. Larger parts of the body, like the legs, were filleted from the body and cooked like a joint of meat, then thrown into dustbins around London. One was found in the dustbin of a branch of McDonald's fast food chain. Most of the body bits were recovered apart from the head.

Nicholas described how he had put the head into a bag, got into his car with his two children, then drove to the Embankment alongside the River Thames and parked his car. He the left the younger child in the car, taking the other child with him to the footbridge that is alongside Hungerford Rail Bridge. When they got to about the middle of the bridge he apparently said to the eldest child, 'Say goodbye to Mummy,' and dropped the bag with her head inside into the river.

About to enter the water to search under a bridge under the River Thames

Setting up to search for Christabel Boyce's head under Hungerford Rail Bridge

When the tide was right we set up a search pattern under the bridge, roughly where Nicholas Boyce said he had dropped the head. We set up a jackstay search from the back of the boat. A jackstay search consists of a line called a shot line, which goes from the boat to a 56lb weight on the riverbed. From that weight there is a line at a pre determined length going to another 56lb weight.

The line is always kept taut and the diver moves along the search line, holding it with one hand and searching with the other. Each time he reaches the weight he moves it an arm's length and continues his search.

This part of the River Thames is tidal so there is a very small window of search at slack water, probably only 20 minutes. Once the tide starts flowing again, even the 56lb weights lift off the bottom. It did not take long to recover the head which was, as Nicholas said, in a shopping bag.

When the pathologist examined Christabel's head, it could be clearly seen there was not just one punch, and Nicholas had cut below marks on her neck that showed she had been strangled with a vacuum cleaner electric cord.

Nicholas Boyce was tried at The Old Bailey in October 1985.

Journalist Maureen Cleave, wrote an article in the London Standard after the trial, described the couple's life prior to the murder, using information she gained by talking to friends and neighbours of Christabel. It was one where Christabel, being the breadwinner of the family tried hard to save an unhappy marriage. She never complained, encouraging Nicholas to do a doctorate at the London School of Economics, and supporting him when his grant ran out, for he was always in trouble with his tutor or his thesis.

Christabel worked as a geriatric social worker to pay his tuition fees, as well as everything else needed by the family. For nearly all their married life she was the sole provider and even had the flat in her name.

Christabel wanted to live in the country, which her husband refused to do, so she finally decided to leave him and take the children with her. She had a house in Lavenham, but worried how Nicholas would manage by himself, and agreed against her better judgement to spend Christmas 1984 with him. Even so, there were signs that she feared for her life. She wrote to an aunt, saying she feared Nicholas was planning to murder her.

Two close friends of Christabel told the reporter they had asked to give evidence at The Old Bailey but were never called. They would have told the court how worried they were about Christabel, and how they begged Christabel to spend Christmas with them. How too, their telephone calls to her would end abruptly when apparently Nicholas came into the room; how she was frightened; how she had brought a few possessions to them in a box for safe keeping, because he had started to break things that were precious to her. He began with her watch.

They also said how Nicholas had been reading books about criminal law and, more disturbingly, about cot deaths.

Nicholas Boyce's defence at his trial, was that his wife was an impossible woman to live with, a nag who provoked him into killing her. His barrister, Michael Wolkind, described his client as 'an exceptionally calm, patient and kind man who finally snapped and lost control.'

Nicholas Boyce was found guilty of the lesser charge of manslaughter, and sentenced to 6 years in prison.

The Judge, Sir James Miskin said on sentencing Boyce, 'Before these dreadful events you were hard working, of good character, devoted to your children and a good father.
You were simply unable to get on with your wife.
You stand convicted of manslaughter.

I will deal with you on the basis you were provoked, you lost your self-control, and that a man of reasonable self-control might have been similarly provoked and might have done what you did.

Not only did you kill her, but you came to your senses, and took meticulous steps to ensure her death would never be discovered. You got rid of her body; you cleaned up the flat as best you could. You cut her up with a saw and boiled her skin and bones. You bagged up her pieces, and over the next two days disposed of her body.'

Boyce was later released early for good behaviour and married his social worker.

I will leave you to decide what you think about this case. I know what my thoughts are and have left the worst to last in my book.

I hope the stories I have selected in my book give you a feel of what it was like to be a Metropolitan Police Diver In the 1980/90s

My thanks to the following people in writing this book

Janet Chard for proof reading.

My wife Kay for supporting me in the bad times I experienced in my life as a police diver.

My two girls, Lisa and Natasha, for being understanding, following my diving career on television, and recording news items for me.

All my colleagues with whom I worked, and who helped

me stay alive, during the 13 years I served in the Metropolitan Police Underwater Search Unit.

Dedicated to the Police divers who were my friends and did not make it, always in my thoughts they are:

Richard (Dick) Amas USU Met Police

Mark Peers USU Met Police

Steve Taylor USU Essex Police

Andrew Morrison USU Essex Police

Other books by Mackenzie Moulton

Poems in my Life

Poems in my in my Life 2

Poems about Brixham

Poems about Wapping (with paintings by the author)

London Police divers log book

Paintings by Artist Mackenzie Moulton

Mac the life

The Lelli Kelly Magic shoes

50 shades of Blue

Seville and Domingo

William Mackenzie, a new beginning

All available on Amazon Books

Self portrait, called 'The standby Diver'

The painting is now on permanent display in the Thames Police Association Museum, Wapping, London.

As well as being an author I am also an artist and musician, I did many paintings when off duty, which at times was a pleasant distraction from some of the stresses of my work.

On retirement I emigrated to Spain, and became a full time artist, both displaying my art for sale, and teaching to the international community where I lived in Javea.

My wife Kay and I lived there for 9 years, but eventually returned, as both our mothers contracted cancer, and a year later Kay's mum died, followed by her father 11 days later, then a few months after that my mum died.

Although we loved Spain, it was the right decision to make, a new chapter in our life, back in the UK

I no longer paint but my work can be seen here

https://fineartamerica.com/profiles/mackenzie-moulton

Printed in Great Britain
by Amazon